Animal Communication

Heart-to-Heart Telepathic Communication with Animals

Revised March 31, 2014

Laurie Moore, PhD, CHT, LMFT, Animal Communicator

831-477-7007

Laurie@DrLaurieMoore.com

www.animiracles.com

ISBN-13: 978-1489515193
ISBN-10: 1489515194

Cover Design Mike De Give

Table of Contents

Introduction	3
Review of Literature	16

Chapter 1:
The Process

A. Understanding	37
B. Initiating Interaction	40
C. Self-Doubt	45
D. Continuing the Conversation	50
E. Finding Your Innate Intuitive Abilities	51
F. Synchronicity	55
G. Stay Open to Others' Differences	58
H. Rituals with Emotional Value	61
I. Speaking with Animals Passed Over	67
J. Counter Transference or Duality Reality	73

Chapter 2:
Animals as Shaman, Shawoman, Teachers and Guides

A. Divine Teachers	80
B. Whales	84
C. Dolphins	87
D. Individuality and Species-ality	90
E. Reincarnation as Initiation	91
Chapter 3: Animals as Caretakers	96
Chapter 4: Animals as Messengers	101
Chapter 5: Animals as Rescuers	106
Chapter 6: Animals as Advisors	110
Chapter 7: Animals as Buddhas	112
Chapter 8: Animals as Mentors to People and Animals	114
Chapter 9: Animals Not Honored	116
Chapter 10: Animals Honored	118
Chapter 11: Animal Emotions	123
Chapter 12: Insects	125
Chapter 13: Life of the Body Ending	127
Chapter 14: Animals Healing from Trauma	130
Chapter 15: Animals Speaking Out loud	132
Chapter 16: Missing Animals Who Leave Home	133
Chapter 17: Rescued Animals	135
Chapter 18: Animals Receiving Healing	137
Chapter 19: Animals Giving Healing	139

Chapter 20
Behavioral and Emotional Challenges

A. Assume Altruism is at Play	140
B. Maintain a Positive Perspective of Inquiry	141
C. Create Solution-Oriented Topics	144
D. Body Needs and Genetic Wiring	144
E. Emotional Learnings	146
F. Spiritual Passages for All Involved	147
G. Mental Frameworks in Transition	148
Chapter 21: Wild Animals	149
Chapter 22: Cross-Species Animal Friends	152
Addendum: Previews from *The Cat's Reincarnation (Moore, 2013)*	155
The Yellow-Winged Peace Moth	156
Red-tailed Hawk Day	157
Conclusion	170
Message from Feline Jessie Justin Joy	171
Introductory Techniques and Exercises	174
Bibliography	199

Introduction

Currently popular in Western cultures, animal communication has been experienced as a normal part of life for centuries in some cultural groups. Practiced hundreds of years back by Mayans, Romani Gypsies, benevolent witches and American Indians among others, animal communication is new to many but not new historically. Perhaps this is why so many people feel that it is innate to them. For many years, children of Western cultures have been apt to report hearing animals and angels talk, but then are told they are imagining things. Others long to better hear their animals but are not sure how. The way is now being made popular so that all people can learn animal communication. Animal communicators, authors, television, the internet, and most importantly, animals themselves, are making this possible.

At the beginning of the twenty-first century, debuting into mainstream culture through Sonya Fitzpatrick's television show *The Pet Psychic (2002–2003)*, the concept of animal communication suddenly became understandable as normal in place of paranormal. Taught for decades in the USA by pioneer in the field, author, and wise elder on animal communication, Penelope Smith (*Animal

Talk, 1999), animal communication focuses on perceiving the messages of animals telepathically, heart to heart. Penelope's work has trained hundreds of communicators and helped the messages of many animal communicators throughout the globe to be heard. Penelope's magazine, *Species Link (1991...current)*, has given a voice to numerous animal communicators and animals. Animals are alert communicators, expressing themselves with telepathic pictures, feelings, and words that emanate in vibration, available for humans to receive.

Those who practice animal communication tend to share one common belief: animal communication is based on heart to heart telepathy. Animals share themselves by sending out pictures, feelings, thoughts, colors, and tones which anyone can learn to comprehend. According to Penelope Smith, "All living creatures have the ability to think, feel, and communicate although most people have forgotten this. Animals around us are sending us messages all the time." Animals speak via intention and qualities of unconditional love. Rather than judging what is, they express awareness of what is.

Awakened gurus such as Ammachi, Ramana Maharshi, Paramahansa Yogananda, and Eckhart Tolle live or have lived lives of communion with animals via respect and mutual communication. *Ammachi: A Biography of Mata*

Amritanandamayi (2002) states that Ammachi regularly received milk from a neighbor's cow who would leave her people, run across town and offer Ammachi her udder fully of her own initiative. Ammachi has been filmed with an elephant blessing her via a dance and the unusual movements of the elephant's trunk. A pig followed Ammachi up to her bedroom and a dove sat on her finger. The animals demonstrated their feelings of love. Ramana Maharshi and Paramahansa Yogananda were known for treating animals as friends and equals. Disciples observed animals to become astute in their presence. St. Francis is known solely for treating animals as brothers and sisters, speaking to them in prayer. Eckhart Tolle said, "I live with three enlightened Zen masters who are all cats."

It is my experience that animals who are treated as equals will reveal themselves to be highly intelligent and spiritually awake. At an Animiracle Satsang (A Gathering in conscious universal love with all species held by The Love Climate, hosting Dr. Laurie Moore as facilitator: www.Animiracles.com), Clare Strohman who had participated for years stood up and said, "In Mexico Dr. Laurie told us that a raven was our sister and was talking to us. Then I watched Laurie wave to the raven and the raven waved back. I realized Laurie is telling the truth."

Tom Kornbluh shared, "I attended a solo retreat with Dr. Laurie and witnessed birds coming to sit with us. When we went inside, they followed." I attribute this to the world community of many species. As we realize that animals are brilliant, they share their brilliance. They join us in gatherings, prayers, and conversations. In this sharing and witnessing, we are able to find out who they really are. What Tom and Clare witnessed may become common place as more and more people realize that animals are our intelligent brothers and sisters. Perhaps a day will come in which viewing animals as less wise or worthy will seem as peculiar as doing so with people of color, women, and people of gay or lesbian life styles. For a long time, people of these qualities were mistakenly seen as less.

When my family moved twenty miles I was sad to leave two raven friends who spoke to me daily. One of them regularly did three flips over my head as a greeting to me. This raven couple was able to find us in our new home. Once they relocated us, the husband presented his three usual flips over my head to affirm it was them.

J. Allen Boone, hired to train Strongheart, a film star German Shepherd, quickly learned that Strongheart was teacher to him. In his book *Kinship with All Life* (1954), he noted that Strongheart communicated with him as an equal when treated as such but became more dog-like when treated like a dog by societal definitions. Boone wrote: "the more we began functioning like rational companions, the more kinship barriers between us came tumbling down." Boone credits Strongheart with reaching Boone telepathically even though Boone had not anticipated this or realized it was possible prior to their meeting.

Dean Bernal, Field Director and founder of the Turks and Caicos Humpback Whale Research Project, became globally recognized for swimming daily with his best friend, JoJo the dolphin, for twenty years. When I interviewed Dean, I learned that JoJo could read Dean's mind. Dean explained, "If I was hungry and wanted a meal, JoJo would take off to get a lobster, come back and present the lobster as a gift to me. As soon as I had a thought, JoJo knew. When I left the islands, JoJo would disappear from the beach for months. Each time I returned, JoJo would return to greet me on the day of my arrival." According to Bernal, Boone, and a vast array of animal communicators, animals hear our thoughts, feel our feelings, and see our imaginings. They can help us remember to retrieve our innate abilities to communicate telepathically heart to heart.

Carol Gurney, author of *The Language of Animals: 7 Steps to Communicating with Animals* (2001), asserts that people communicate telepathically all day long. We don't need to learn how. We simply need to recognize we are doing this and validate it. Learning to talk to animals who are domestic, wild, on Earth, and passed over is available to all people. You can learn Spanish, French, Japanese, or languages from numerous African countries and you can learn to speak to animals. In *Animal Voices* (Bear & Company, 2002), animal communicator Dawn Baumann Brunke explains that we are actually receiving messages from animals and from each other all the time. Penelope Smith, Dawn Baumann Brunke, and Carol Gurney, all accomplished animal communicators and authors, maintain the belief that animal communication is a process of recognizing innate abilities one already has. Often, people who come to the Animiracles Satsangs express that they hear my cat Jessie speaking to them and that they are not used to cats speaking to them. I believe that they are able to hear Jessie because they have walked into an environment in which Jessie's speaking is validated and considered quite natural. Once they honor this in themselves, within a supportive environment, they can re-find this ability with other animals anywhere and any time.

There has been a belief permeating many cultures that animals are a lesser species. Simultaneously, many people have silently realized that animals are masters of unconditional love, joy, peace, and compassion; the qualities that all religions espouse to emulate! Now, animals are gaining more respect and honor for their intelligence, wisdom, and spiritually evolved presences. I sometimes imagine a global community government with animals included in professional roles. Of course this will require society waking up to our ability to communicate telepathically. As I witness this awakening occurring more and more, for larger numbers of people every day, I witness the joy and wisdom that unfolds in humans. I deeply experience this firsthand at the Animiracles Satsangs. I hear of more and more people experiencing such in their sacred communities. Examples of communities with great respect for animal wisdom include Perelandra Center for Nature Research in Virginia, Paws and Claws Private Sanctuary in California, Findhorn in Scotland, Penelope Smith's Buffalo Spirit Lodge in Prescott, Arizona, and Dolphinville on the Big Island of Hawaii to name a few).

Gina Palmer, animal communicator and author of the "Paws & Claws Newsletter" (2001–2006), studied with Mayan elder Hunbatz Men. She reported when I spoke to her, "The Mayans believed that people who awakened could come back as animals, a wiser species." Hunbatz, in his article "Living on the Edge of a New World" (http://www.labyrinthina.com/mayan.htm)), elaborates that essence and spirit are one and arrive on the planet before species in form. Animal, plant, human, and element as energy essence came first and the physical representation appears later. When animals are missing from an environment, so are the good spirits; and death will potentially come to Earth. In Mayan culture, animals are to be honored and respected as sacred members of the community.

Takatoka of Manataka American Indian Council explains that animal communication takes place via telepathy and spirit. (See www.manataka.org/page291.html)

Gina Palmer speaks of a coyote who was personally invited to an elder circle ceremony and then showed up. I invited a cat I met at summer camp to meet me in cabin #15 when I was a girl and the cat, PJ, knocked on our door fifteen minutes later. When I opened it, he came in and jumped on my bed. Another time, when I was a student in England, I wished a cat would visit me. Within 24 hours a loving cat came into the house and greeted me on my bed. Animals hear our thoughts from close and far.

I invited animals to be my teachers at the private Hidden Valley Sanctuary in Soquel, CA by sending out a message from my heart to the surrounding environment. For my entire three and a half years there, I was approached by hawks, ravens, hummingbirds, deer, dogs, coyote, bobcats, frogs, owls, goldfinches, bees, and lizards who worked deeply with me as Shaman/Shawoman, teaching me of inner worlds, other dimensions and unconditional love, oneness and reverence. You can read about this in detail in my book *The Cat's Reincarnation and Unconditional Trust in Love* (2006).

Recognizing one's innate ability to communicate with animals can come in many ways. Some are more adept at hearing while others at seeing or feeling. Some people feel emotions while some feel inspired energies. Some also see waves of lights and colors or hear tones that emanate from people, plants, and animals. Some are graced with a combination of all of these communication aspects. As individual animals also have tendencies toward particular communication emphasis (thoughts, pictures, emotions, inspired feelings, waves of color and light, tones), the communication between a person and an animal is an art just as the communication between two people is an art.

If you were to put a vase of flowers in the middle of a room, surround the flowers with twelve people, give each person the best camera available and ask them to click, what would happen? You would see twelve different pictures of the same bouquet. Each picture would be accurate. So, with communication between any two beings there is a subjective artistry. However, there is also a science. Each bouquet photograph would also share common traits with all others and a similar essence. In the same way, if twelve skilled animal communicators speak to a dog, they will each share what the dog said in a way that represents their own uniqueness. However, there will also be a common message from the dog that everyone will hear.

Doubt is very common among people beginning to speak to animals. For this reason, asking the animals to validate that you are actually receiving their messages is important. They will find ways to help you in this regard. When I studied animal communication with Gina Palmer, a white cat began to show up at my therapy session with my clients. The white cat was clear to me but not embodied. She would assist me with the clients. I described her to Gina Palmer who sent me a photo of her cat Sno, who she had not previously mentioned. I recognized the photo at once! Sno had found a way to contact me. When Sno and I first met in body, Sno came to sit with me. Gina said she had been avoiding people and even hissing at them. Sno validated that our long distance communion was mutually felt in her immediate familiarity with me. Sno helped me to trust that my tuning in to her was not imagined.

Another way to address doubt is to speak to human families of animals. If you hear an animal giving you information, ask the animal permission to talk to one of his or her people. When people tell you that what you heard the animal say is true, you will begin to believe yourself. For example, an animal may tell you something personal about a person in a very nonjudgmental way. You might share this with the person and because it was their trusted animal companion who said it, they might feel safe to say, "Yes that is true," feeling secure in disclosing something that had been previously embarrassing. They may recognize that you had no other way of knowing what the animal friend told you. Then your faith in your own way of hearing, feeling, and seeing what animals are saying will grow.

Sonya Fitzpatrick was filmed for television in *The Pet Psychic (2002–2003)* talking to an alligator who shared a secret that his human caretaker and friend had confided in only him. His caretaker had told the alligator that the alligator was the best show man in the lake and had also told the alligator that he, the caretaker, was having marriage problems. The alligator reported all this to Sonya who mentioned it to the caretaker. When the caretaker heard what Sonya said, trust was established. Sonya had no other means of knowing this personal communication that had been shared between caretaker and alligator.

The reason that the caretaker had originally contacted Sonya was because his alligator friend stopped doing tricks at the alligator park. The caretaker wanted to find out why and what to do to remedy this. The alligator told Sonya he would resume his tricks when his red meat diet was resumed. The diet had been recently replaced with something less favorable for his health but this was not public information. Sonya would not have known this from another source. Sonya let the caretaker know. The alligator's caretaker went back to giving his alligator friend the old red meat diet upon receiving Sonya's guidance. The alligator immediately returned to performing. This validated Sonya's communicating. While Sonya had communicated with hundreds of animals and did not need validation, the example shows you that validation will come when you are accurate.

While people in modern culture have learned to place a strong line between what we know as life and what we call "death," animals know all animals and people to be eternal. The leaving of the body is like the leaving of some clothes one wears temporarily. As one takes off the supporting costume, the soul goes on. As a result, speaking to animals who are on the other side is done in the same way as speaking to animals who are embodied. *Animals in Spirit* (2008) by Penelope Smith gives numerous accounts of animals communicating to humans from the afterlife. Animals are happy to talk to people with or without bodies. They will talk to us from their domestic abodes, from their wild habitats and from the world beyond the physical.

As we allow the intellect to serve the universal heart, which beats through all beings, in many voices, we begin to hear, feel and see the communications of animals. As we do this, we learn to better attune to our sister and brother humans from the heart. We begin to honor and know each other as souls and waves of energy, here to share love.

While this book will focus on telepathic communication, the author wishes to equally validate the role of studying the behavior and physical body language of animals. As Temple Grandin emphasizes in *Animals In Translation* (2005), animals' many keenly sharpened senses, perception of details, and physical abilities, which are not shared by humans, contribute to how animals perceive and interact with the world. One who is adept at telepathic communication will deepen and expand his/her understanding and interactions with animals by learning the physical realities of a species. Some of this can come via telepathic communication, some through observation, and some through study of others' findings.

This book will discuss methods, experiences, and case examples of conscious telepathic communication occurring between people and animals. People and animals who have contributed to this field will be included in this discussion. This book will help you to understand how to communicate with animals of any species who are either living with you, located near or far away, or passed over. This book will give you many inspiring case examples of humans' experiences of animal communication. From reading this book and working with practices offered, you may come to understand that animals are wise teachers, shaman, healers, and deeply committed co-members of your community, which is a multi-species globe. You may find yourself in a deeper heart place with an ever greater awe and respect for all of life. I know that you, who choose to read this book, are already of the heart and conscious soul.

Review of Literature

Those of you who are familiar with my other books including *The Cat's Reincarnation: Transformative Encounters with Animals (2013),* and *Healing and Awakening the Heart: Animal Wisdom for Humans,* know my writing style. It's personal and metaphorical. For this one book I take a different road. Here I celebrate a plethora of communicators. Animal Communication is something we can learn about from many.

Animal Voices: Telepathic Communication in the Web of Life (2002) by Dawn Baumann Brunke offers a respectful portrayal of animals from a variety of animal species. Dawn contributes the viewpoints of a variety of animals as well as authors and animal communicators to help readers develop an empathetic understanding of animals' viewpoints. Dawn allows her book to be a vehicle through which dogs, birds, cats, fish, dolphins, and other animal species share their emotions, opinions, spirituality, and soul reasons for incarnating onto Earth.

Animal Voices, Animal Guides: Discover Your Deeper Self through Communication with Animals (2009) by Dawn Baumann Brunke invites the reader into great understanding of his or her own intuitive capabilities. Dawn supports readers in communicating with animals as a means of developing greater connection with one's own benevolent self. This book is filled with advice from animal communication professionals as well as animals. Many species are included from sled dogs to llamas. Games, exercises, and experiments are given to help the reader gain a deeper sensing of the voices of animals.

Shapeshifting With Our Animal Companions: Connecting with the Spiritual Awareness of All Life (2008) by Dawn Baumann Brunke tells us that shapeshifting with animals into various aspects of consciousness is possible. In letting go, opening to experience and integrating awareness we merge with animal wisdom, thus finding new awareness within ourselves. As the reader comes to remember life and death as a shifting-of-form event rather than an end all, a new comprehension of who we are as consciousness may be born.

Dolphin Notes: Insights from My First Summer with the Dolphins (2008) by Meg Sibley shares her experiences of love, peace, and delight during her dolphin swims. Accepting them as teachers of heart, she offers the gifts she receives from dolphins to her readers.

Dolphins Into the Future (1997) by Joan Ocean is a true journey into the lives of dolphins who inhabit numerous paradigms. Joan offers her experiences of befriending and swimming with dolphins who share colors, lights, and Shamanic invitations into bliss and light realms. Joan shares many experiences of being approached, invited, and initiated by dolphins into realms of awakening and love. This book confirms that communication with animals is a natural extension of offering a heart as a witness and offering one's self for experience via trust.

Animal Talk: Interspecies Telepathic Communication (1999; re-released 2008) by Penelope Smith gives detailed information on how to communicate with animals. Penelope helps readers develop and discover their innate ability to communicate with animal friends. She addresses behavior problems in interspecies families with solutions that honor both animal and human needs. This book teaches you to open your heart to the hearts, souls, and minds of animal friends.

When Animals Speak: Techniques for Bonding with Animal Companions (2009) by Penelope Smith, offers profound life-altering illumination given directly from animals. Animals express their feelings about Earth life, humans, and their personal paths. Animals convey the depth of their spiritual understandings and intentions. They contribute their own perspectives on how they teach, heal, and guide people into wholeness and balance.

When Elephants Weep: The Emotional Lives of Animals (1995) by Jeffrey Moussaieff Masson and Susan McCarthy gives personal experiences of people who have lived with animals in the wild. These people come to appreciate the emotional lives these animals experience. Jeffrey and Susan are able to point out the ways in which humans and animals are precisely the same in terms of tender experience. Introducing us to buffalo, chimpanzee, gorilla, crows, and a parrot, Jeffery and Susan bring the readers heart-to-heart recognition that animals are our sisters and brothers.

Cat Miracles: Inspirational True Stories of Remarkable Felines (2003) by Brad Steiger and Sherry Hansen Steiger volunteers numerous true stories from many people and their beloved cats. This book gives evidence that cats are highly intelligent beings, capable of far more than most realize. Cats can find their own way from one location to another hundreds of miles away. This book helps people to understand that cats' capacities for understanding their world are vast and full of genius.

Animal Miracles: Inspirational and Heroic True Stories (1999) by Brad Steiger and Sherry Hansen Steiger is a collection of true stories shared by people regarding their heroic animal companions. Animals who behave as selfless servants, angels, and great ambassadors of profound love are announced.

The Compassion of Animals: True Stories of Animal Courage and Kindness (1997) by Kristin von Kreisler introduces the reader to numerous animals who chose spontaneous compassion and service as their way of life. True accounts of animals who risked their own lives to protect their human beloveds from harm are discussed. The selfless courage and deep love animals give to their human families becomes evident.

Ammachi: A Biography of Mata Amritanandamayi (1994) by Swami Amritaswarupananda includes a variety of relationships the Indian Saint and Guru, Ammachi, co-creates with animal beloveds. Animals' profound love, willingness to share love, choices to serve in love, and great ability to communicate love are honored in this book.

Ramana Maharshi and the Path of Self-Knowledge: A Biography (2006) by Arthur Osborn includes an entire chapter on Ramana's communication with animals. This book explains Ramana was surrounded by animals with whom he communicated as friends. Ramana's understanding of his animal friends was that they, like humans, were there to work off karma and to awaken. He knew animals to be fully capable of complete liberation. In this book, a variety of true episodes are presented in which wild animals trust, befriend, treat humans well, and show complete understanding of Ramana's communications to them.

Cat Talk: The Secrets of Communicating with Your Cat (2003) by Sonya Fitzpatrick describes a plethora of interactions between herself and cats. The cats teach us that resolution to life challenges begins with mutual respect and communication. In shedding illumination on solutions to animal health problems, family emotional problems, and animal mood problems, the value of communication between people and animals is made clear.

Animals in Spirit: Our Faithful Companions' Transition to the Afterlife (2008) by Penelope Smith expands communication with animals into the topic of death and birth. Extending true conversations between person and animal on topics of passing over and reincarnation, Penelope shows us that animals' viewpoint on death is different than many humans. Surrendering to death as a normal part of life, understanding when it is time, and sometimes reincarnating, animals stay in great harmony with source as they journey in this way.

Essential Joy: Finding It, Keeping It, Sharing It: Book 1: The Art of Balance (2002) by Trish Regan explores the personal transformation from despair to joy that Trish has discovered. Through her communing with the dolphins as her sisters, brothers, and guides she finds states of unconditional joy and love. This book gives you exercises to find this joy yourself.

Essential Joy: Finding It, Keeping It, Sharing It: Book 2: Surrender to Magnificence (2002) by Trish Regan continues the journey into unconditional joy initiated in *Essential Joy: Finding It, Keeping It, Sharing It: Book 1.* The reader is offered exercises designed to take them even further into the core of their own joy. This book is inspired by Trish's teachers, guides, and family, the dolphins.

The Language of Animals: 7 Steps to Communicating with Animals (2008) by Carol Gurney gives heart-based steps for animal communication. This book includes exercises for the reader as well as stories of Carol's experiences with animals. It also presents tools for overcoming communication breakdowns and finding solutions to behavior problems. In addition, this book lists tips for reconnecting with lost animals, finding lost animals, and facing the death of a beloved animal companion.

Animals as Teachers and Healers (1996; 1997) by Susan Chernak McElroy shares how her wellness overcomes her cancer due to the love of animals in her life. She goes on to let the reader know of more true stories of humans who have been touched and changed from animals' love and healing energies. This book takes people into depths of joy, wisdom, and healing that are born via relationships between people and beloved animals.

Animals In Translation: Using the Mysteries of Autism to Decode Animal Behavior (2005) by Temple Grandin with Catherine Johnson draws on Grandin's own life experience with autism as well as her career as an animal scientist to give illuminated understanding of how animals think, act and feel. She is able to bridge telepathic animal communication and understanding of genetic behavior.

Animal Speak (1993) by Ted Andrews indicates that particular animals may be crossing a person's path when a particular teaching is being invoked. Ted suggests that each species has a certain set of traits and wisdoms. When a person is to benefit from using a species' innate talents, or from releasing a habit, it is possible that an animal from that species will appear to the person in body. This book serves as guidance for better understanding the potential reasons why a particular animal has been in your world.

The Pet Whisperer: Stories About My Friends, the Animals (2003) by Stephen R. Blake, DVM, is a book about a holistic veterinarian's experiences with animals. Dr. Blake, who learned both Western and Eastern medicine, mainstream and alternative modalities, exuberantly relates his passages with his animal friends. His communication with the animals is the crux of his ability to assist their healing. The delight that the animals' people receive when animals heal emotionally and physically is touching.

Behaving As If the God in All Life Mattered (1997) by Machaelle Small Wright is a divine account of a human working in communication with insects. In order to grow a healthy garden, Machaelle learns to speak to the spirits who govern insect life.

Kinship with All Life (1954) by J. Allen Boone is the true story of Allen's surprise learning excursions with a canine and a fly who take him in as their disciple.

The Souls of Animals (1991) by Gary Kowalski is a fulfilled effort to awaken people to the reality that animals have souls. This book assists the reader in recognizing that animals have feelings, wisdom, artistry, awareness, inspired intentions, divine qualities, and intelligence. Gary challenges human doubts in animals' ascended realities as cultural misinterpretations coming from people who attempt to understand animals without putting themselves in the animals' shoes first.

Animals Make Us Human; Creating the Best Life for Animals (2009) by Temple Grandin with Catherine Johnson gives insights so that readers can give animals the best and happiest life possible. This is offered on the animals' terms instead of the humans' terms. Grandin explains core emotional needs of animals. She explains how to support the fulfillment of these needs for domestic and zoo animals.

Communication with All Life: Revelations of an Animal Communicator (2007) by Joan Ranquet is a book for people who do not perceive themselves to be telepathic and wish to learn. Joan did not comprehend herself to be an animal intuitive as a child. She learned. She says she learned in many ways from coming to recognize what she was already doing and giving this more direction and focus. She says that we all have intuitive gifts so you can do this too. Her book takes your hand and helps walk you down the path of learning your own way of animal communication.

We Borrow the Earth: An Intimate Portrait of the Gypsy Shamanic Tradition and Culture (2000) by Patrick Jasper Lee draws on biographical adventures of Patrick's own life, growing up as a Romani Gypsy. He was taught that his relationship to his horse was his responsibility. If his horse was not riding well with him it was due to Patrick's need to improve his attunement and communication. Patrick was also taught that a guardian ancestor could re-appear as an animal. He was raised to see himself in reverence to the Earth and the Earths' creatures. This view point can be an eye opener to modern man who has learned to control and conquer the earth. Patrick was speaking with animals as a norm as were the other children in his community from a young age.

The Future is Yours: Do Something About it (2003) by Raymon Grace is an exploration of the energies that compose realities. Our human ability to shift realities on this planet, both near and far, via our relating to them is made clear. Working together for the benefit of all, healing illness, and restoring harmony is the invitation of this book. Tools for doing so are offered.

Exploring the Levels of Creation by Sylvia Brown (2006) is a psychic's perception of reality. Her experiences are relevant to those embarking upon a professional path of animal intuitive.

Learning Their Language: Intuitive Communication with Animals and Nature (2003) by Marta Williams teaches readers how to talk with animals by providing instructions and exercises. This book also includes approaches to addressing accuracy and verification. The pages are filled with true stories sent to Marta from her clients who discovered their ability to communicate with animals via her teachings.

Beyond Words: Talking with Animals and Nature (2005) by Marta Williams is a collection of true stories from many people who have experienced intuitive communication with animals. Included are pivotal points in peoples' lives in which animals convinced them that animal communication is real. Another section focuses on animal training. A chapter about transformational life moments in which animals inspire a new spiritual understanding in humans is also part of this book.

Ask Your Animal: Resolving Behavioral Issues Through Intuitive Communication (2008) by Marta Williams is a guide for utilizing intuitive communication with animals to solve behavior problems. Step-by-step practices, exercises, and true stories are all part of this educational book. Some of the topics addressed are restoring trust after an animal has been violated by humans, helping animals in a family to get along, transforming aggressive actions, supporting sick and injured animals, and connecting with animals who are in crisis or who were rescued.

The Cat's Reincarnation: Transformative Encounters with Animals (2013) by Laurie Moore invites us into the universal world of unconditional love, peace, and joy. Taking the reader into Shamanic transformational journeys created via animal and person union, this book is an experiential read. As animals teach Laurie to return to love, gratitude, and surrender in each moment, bliss is revealed.

Animiracles (2007) by Laurie Moore is a DVD that places focus on animals' roles as teachers. The DVD begins with Tory, the dog, who was running away from his person frequently. When Laurie asks Tory why, Tory explains that his person is running from his own heart. Tory tells Laurie that when Dr. Bell comes home to his own heart, Tory will stop running. Dr. Bell, Tori's person tries out the advice and finds out it works. As the DVD continues, we encounter a woman who is unable to meet a horse on the horse's terms and tries to talk to him in intellectual and psychological terminology of the mind. The horse runs or snorts. When the woman locates her own heart as the central point for communication, and speaks to Décor, the horse, heart to heart, Décor becomes loving and full of kisses and hugs to share.

Indimiracles (2007) by Laurie Moore is a DVD designed to teach the viewer intentional artistry in life as inspired by animals and humans. The premise of this DVD is that intention, surrender and love are the basis of all our experiences. The exercises and sharing gifted through this DVD guide the way to joy, happiness, and fulfillment.

111 Messages to Humanity (2007) by Jessie Justin Joy is a book written by a cat. This book gives humanity insightful advice on how to awaken spiritually in a practical world by using all situations as opportunities for awareness and love.

Prayer to Our Animal Friends (c. early 1200s: exact date unknown) by St. Francis of Assisi is a prayer that makes St. Francis relationship to animals as companions very clear. He addresses animal species as a wonderful gift from God. He asks that the humans' animal companions be relieved of suffering. He acknowledges their trust in the humans and asks that any diseases inflicted on their bodies be removed.

Sermon to the Birds (1220) by St. Francis is an acknowledgement from St. Francis that birds are his siblings. He addresses them as loved ones who can hear. He reminds them to remain in gratitude.

The Holy Bible Old Testament (Job 12: 7–10), a Jewish and once Christian sacred document reminds us that animals can both hear and speak. "Ask the birds, ask the beasts and they will teach you."

The Holy Qur'an (27:16), a Muslim sacred document, tells us that humans had acquired the miracle of speech with animals as early as the time of King Solomon. "And Solomon was David's heir, and he said: 'O ye people! We have been taught the speech of birds...' "

*The Holy Bhagavad Gita (*Bhagavad Gita 5.18) states that animals and humans are equal: "An enlightened person—by perceiving God in all—looks at a learned person, an outcast, a cow, an elephant, or a dog with an equal eye."

Wisdom of the Animals: Communication Between Animals and the People who Love Them (2001) by Raphaela Pope and Elizabeth Morrison imparts stories of animals, answers from animals in interviews, and learning that occurs when people engage in animal communication. This book also addresses how to talk with animals, how to quiet the mind in order to reach animals' worlds, how to face one's doubts in animal communication, and how to allow the process to unfold.

Animal Wisdom: Communications with Animals (1996) by Anita Curtis discusses Anita's personal conversations and excursions with animals, how to communicate with animals, animals who have been lost and found, and the use of dowsing in animal communication.

Blessing the Bridge: What Animals Teach us About Death, Dying, and Beyond (2001) by Rita M. Reynolds is a true journey of saying goodbye to a beloved animal in the physical. Rita, who has worked with hundreds of ill and dying animals, shares her own experience with a beloved dog family member. In this way she is able to support people to be present with their animals' needs and their own needs when physical death is coming.

How to Communicate with Animals—The Basic Course (Audio CD set; 2004) by Penelope Smith is an at-home course. The listener will be taken through exercises to bring them back to an innate ability to speak with animals.

Animal Communication Mastery Series (Audio CD Set; 2006) by Penelope Smith will teach you to break through the layers of conditioning that separates you from your complete connection with animals. The listener will find out that she or he can see, hear, touch, smell, and feel the world through animal beings' perspectives. The listener will find ways to help resolve behavior and emotional issues, illness, and pain. The path for deepening of mutual understanding and cooperation between person and animal will be delivered.

Animal Healing Power (Audio CD; 2008) by Penelope Smith is an offering of clear and inspiring information on who animals really are. The listener will be able to venture into capabilities of helping animals to heal. The listener will also learn to allow animals to help you on your path of self-discovery. This CD encourages reverence for animals and all of life.

Telepathic Communication with Animals (DVD; 2005) by Penelope Smith is an introduction and overview of the subject of animal communication. This one is a great eye-opener for skeptics. Penelope demonstrates ways of increasing comprehension and harmonious conversing with beings from other species. She shows the viewer how to expand abilities to fully communicate with animals. She helps the viewer to regain your innate ability to telepathically be in touch with animals.

Conversations with Animals: Cherished Messages and Memories as Told by an Animal Communicator (1998) by Lydia Hiby with Bonnie S. Weintraub emphasizes the powerful connection between animals and humans. Hiby was born aware of her ability to talk with animals. As she was never discouraged she kept this innate intelligence throughout life. These authors help readers to access their own animal communication ability, find ways to heal from loss and grief, and reunite with missing animal family members.

Echo of the Elephants (PBS and BBC: 1993; DVD: 2006) written and narrated by David Attenborough and Cynthia Moss, filmed and directed by Martyn Colbeck. This documentary film shows anthropologist Cynthia Moss's life right near elephants. Cynthia stayed close to elephants for twenty-five years and gained enough trust to witness their personal and tribal relations and rituals.

Straight from the Horse's Mouth: How to Talk to Animals and Get Answers (2001) by Amelia Kinkade is written by a well-known animal intuitive who did not always believe that animal communication was possible. Inspired and mentored by her cat, Rodney, Amelia became a believer and has now worked with many animals. In her book she offers meditations and exercises created to improve intuition. She discusses how to negotiate compromise in interspecies families. She shows the reader that people and animals can re-find each other in the face of a rift.

Ask the Animals: Life Lessons Learned as an Animal Communicator (2003) by Kim Ogden-Avrutik shows the reader that animals think and feel just as humans do. Touching stories reveal the loving, kind, and compassionate nature of animals. These stories teach that animals arrive in our loves for particular reasons, often as our teachers and guides. Erasing the notion that humans are higher up than animals in any hierarchy, this book humbles the human to respect the animals.

What Animals Tell Me: True Stories of an Animal Communicator (2005) by Monica Deidrich is a sharing of Monica's personal and very heart felt connections with animals. She allows then to teach her. She hears their wishes. She speaks to all kinds of species. This book reads like a novel but speaks of real life.

What Horses Say: How to Hear, Help and Heal Them (2004) by Anna Clemence Mews and Julie Dicker honors horses for their intelligence and ability to observe, think, and reason. Sixty-two horses and ponies are interviewed on their needs and deepest feelings. Julie Dicker is able to provide answers to puzzling challenges and questions that people living with horses face.

Paws & Claws (2001–2006) by Gina Palmer is a newsletter that shares Gina's personal experiences with beloved animal friends (www.pawsandclaws.net). Through adventurous challenges, lessons, and resolutions, Gina prospers greatly from her animal loved ones. These animals serve as spiritual teachers, counselors, healers, and shaman/shawoman. Recognizing the great intentions and skills her animal friends come to impart, she liberates reader and self with her writing.

Talking with the Animals (1998) by Patty Summers asserts that everyone can speak with animals. Patty defines the telepathy that is used between humans and animals as the universal language of the Earth Mother. She explains that telepathy can involve seeing, feeling, and hearing. Patty describes animals' worlds, emphasizing that they share the same needs, wants, and emotions that humans encounter in themselves.

Little Creatures Who Run the World (1998), directed by Nick Upton, is a film that educates the viewer on the elaborate intelligence of ants. This movie teaches people that ants have survived on Earth for three million years via communal-based working and living. Ants, who take up as much weight on the planet as human beings, are survivalists because of their ability to focus on the good of all tribe members at all times.

The Calico Shaman: True Tales of Animal Communication (2004), by Carla Person with Hillary Johnson, creates understanding for readers of the shamanic roles animals play. In sharing her personal trail as the student of animal teachers, she brings readers into new awareness. Readers witness the wise roles animals intentionally play in our spiritual awakening.

The Animal Connection: A Guide to Intuitive Communication with Your Pet (2000) by Judy Meyer hands the reader guidance on how to hear and understand what animal companions are saying. She engages the reader in ways to interact with animals in love, respect, and nurturance, and she assists the process of redirecting undesired behaviors. She also installs confidence in the reader with how to communicate when away from home and apart from a loved animal.

Speak to My Heart: Carla Person's Step-by-step Method for Shamanic Animal Communication (DVD; 2002) by Carla Person shows the viewer a way of approaching animal communication as a shamanic journey. Simple steps are given so that novices can enter the shamanic world with animals.

Tails of a Healer: Animals, Reiki and Shamanism (2008) by Rose De Dan features forty-five true animal stories written over eleven years. Emphasis is on these animals' roles in the life and evolution of the healer who wrote the book. Black-and-white photographs are included.

Angel Animals: Divine Messengers of Miracles (2007) by Allen and Linda Anderson, with a foreword by Dr. Marty Becker DVM, is a collection of stories from people who have learned spiritual lessons and truths from animals. Topics with which animals guide and assist are relationships, life challenges, death, dying, and the afterlife.

Harmonie (CD; 2009) by Roop Verma is transformational meditative music on sitar. This music is created by Roop to harmonize the chakras, the subtle bodies and physical bodies through the use of Nada Yoga. Nada Yoga is a study and awakening into creation via sound vibration.

Magic Cat (an enlightened animal) Explains Creation (2004) is a book of teachings by a feline named Magic Cat. This book was channeled by Yael and Doug Powell. Magic Cat assists people in understanding the awakened state. Magic Cat also brings people into intricate understandings of presence, god, sexuality, death passages, and life values.

Species Link: The Journal of Interspecies Telepathic Communication (1990 to current) is a quarterly magazine written by Penelope Smith and animal communicators from around the world. This magazine is dedicated to featuring the lives of animals, the learning humans receive from animals, and the exploration of important current questions regarding animals.

Chapter 1

The Process

A. Understanding

As the 20th Century has ended and the 21st Century has begun, many humans have become adept at telepathic animal communication and have written books on the topic. Most animal communication teachers and authors agree that communication with animals requires visiting with their eyes, ears, feelings, inspired energies, or physical sensations. This is an act of empathetic witnessing and experiencing at once; putting oneself into another's world. Whether first experienced as an inherent gift or learned via practice, this remains true.

The animal world according to animal experience is not based on comparisons as is the human world of the mind. The animal world of telepathic communicating is based on being present in what is, knowing soul purpose, and having intention aligned with soul purpose. This communication originates in the universal source, moves through the soul and expresses as personality (In this case we should actually say "animal-ality"). For this reason, animals communicate with a nonjudgmental perspective: *How do I help? How do I assist? How do I serve? Here is what is occurring. How do I remain faithful to my source? Here is what is happening.* To fully understand one from the animal kingdom, entering this nonjudgmental zone of presence and intention is necessary.

Sometimes the concept of full presence without comparative judgment is misunderstood by human intellect as a panacea existence in which everything is happy. If we look at the root origin of "happy," which means to occur successively as a stream of varied experiences, this is so. Where humans sometimes fail to look is that this happiness is a peace which can hold all emotions and thoughts rather than eliminate particular emotions and thoughts. So a bird, for example, living in a house with two cats may snuggle with one cat and keep his or her distance from another. A human may think this is a problem and ask the bird, "What is wrong?"

The bird may not understand the concept of something being wrong. Explaining that one cat is sulky and this vibration is not conducive to the bird's enjoyment, the bird may see this as how things are rather than an indication of what is not. In the bird's mind this cat is sulky and is meant to be currently sulky just as this bird is meant to keep distance from this particular cat at this time. In the bird's awareness this does not make anything wrong. While the situation may or may not be altered in some way, the bird is at peace in the deepest sense. While the bird may have emotional feelings about this situation and make decisions based on these feelings, this is all done within a greater unconditional surrender to a deeper presence and peace. Thus, any altering comes from a place of everything being right.

It is important to begin to grasp this distinction in the heart and mind to be able to understand the communication animals have to offer. The human species is trained to create a resistance to circumstances that seem unjust or unfit or non-preferable. While the animal species is capable of changing situations, having deep emotions and many thoughts reflecting the reality of situations, a profound connection to surrendering in heart to what is this moment is the basis. A human learning the language of animals will naturally venture to encounter this level of surrender in self, as a means of connecting with an animal.

Everyone is capable of learning animal communication. Because it is a language of the heart and soul, the process of learning differs from learning a secondary language from another country. It is not an act of memorizing but rather, an act of coming deeper into awareness of one's innate intuitive abilities. Everyone has a set of intuitive abilities that are exercised on a daily basis. Some are more alert to this. Some are more trusting of this. Some have spent time developing this. Those who are less familiar or less conscious of their intuitive abilities do have them.

B. Initiating Interaction

Because animals live in the realms of gratitude, the first step is to take one's own heart into a place of gratitude. Return to a state of appreciation in your own heart to begin. This is done by thinking of something for which one feels thankful or by simply recalling the area in the heart where gratitude dwells unconditionally and eternally. There are a number of ways to do this. Some people think about circumstances and loved ones that naturally bring them back to gratitude. Some are able to locate gratitude simply by focusing on the heart's love. Some say a mantra, put on a piece of music that brings forth appreciation, or pull a memoir out of a file. Some go to a place they have designated indoors, outdoors, or in their imagination as an environment of thanks. You will find and know the best way for you.

Once one is in a state of gratitude s/he can approach an animal by focusing his/her heart on the animal's heart. Feel into one's heart and bring this to the animal. Give gratitude to the animal. This can be done by sending a feeling message or a picture or a thought or a sound that centers on gratitude. Send your appreciation to this animal. The animal will immediately feel it. Because all animals are aware of their natural heart telepathy, your message is as tangible and visceral to an animal as an email or phone call is to you. Some of you, who already live in the realm of heart-to-heart telepathy, know that you are aware of others when they think of you. This is the same for almost all animals.

After sending gratitude, invite the animal to dialogue with you. Ask the animal if s/he is available to be in a conversation with you. In the same way that you ask a friend out to lunch, you ask a friend when a good time to call might be, you ask your wife if she would like to go for a walk, you ask an animal if s/he is available to talk. In the same way that you honor a "yes" or "no" from a human, you honor the animal's answer. The majority of the time, animals are willing to talk and are happy to do so. However, sometimes it is not an appropriate time for them as they must focus elsewhere. Respect the answer you receive, which will come in one or more of the following: pictures, words, sounds, emotional feelings, colors, lights, physical sensations, scents, or inspired feelings.

Animals can talk while playing, sleeping, eating, and doing just about anything else. Animals assume that being in communication is an ongoing part of being alive and not something that is necessary to be cut off because one is engaged in a physical situation.

If you receive a "yes" about dialoguing, take your focus to the animal's world. In order to understand the animal in terms of his or her own self-understanding, ask "what is your soul purpose?" This will allow you to begin with respect and reverence for the animal rather than imposed ideas about the animal. Animals are very to the point and in the moment. There is never a need to beat around the bush or share small talk. Intellectual complexities designed by human species are likely to disinterest an animal as they are working with pure authenticity. Because animals find their strengths and weaknesses to be equally valid and acceptable, they have little to hide. If they have not been punished or educated to feel unworthy, they tend to share in an innocent and straightforward manner. For example, a rabbit may say, I am very nosey and extremely wise. My mate, Dennis, is deeply nurturing and also clumsy. The rabbit may report this to you matter-of-factly. In her eyes, nosey, extremely wise, deeply nurturing, and clumsy are all valid. No fear of boasting and no fear of being judged for a weakness are present. To the rabbit, it is natural that each individual has a variety of traits. This is obvious and nothing to be secretive about.

Once you ask an animal about soul purpose, you will again receive information in one or more of the following: pictures, words, sounds, emotional feelings, colors, lights, physical sensations, scents, or inspired feelings. What you receive will be based on that particular animal's orientation as well as yours. So if the animal is more of a talker than a visualist you will receive more words than pictures. However if you are more of a visualist than a talker you may be more attentive to pictures. Make a point to notice all of the messages coming in all ways so that you can be more adept at receiving this particular animal. If that is challenging, it is something to work with. It need not stop you from communicating.

In some cases, someone is wired up in a particular mode (i.e. auditory, visual, somatic, energetic, intuitive, etc.) and simply isn't able to move into other modes, even with practice. This need not block communication as there is a natural universal translation system as well as the help of the spirits when gratitude and the heart remain the basis of connecting. In other words, if your visual nature is not letting you hear an animal's words, universal source can find ways to translate his or her words into pictures for you. This can occur with any two modes. Somatic messages can be turned to auditory ones, visual messages can be turned to somatic ones, and so forth. However, in the same way that you will find it more natural to communicate with particular people due to your wiring and their's being more aligned, you may find it more natural to communicate with particular animals. You and particular animals may have an affinity for one another and be naturally drawn into each other's lives. This being said, there is still plenty of room to connect with everyone in some way, experiencing some of who that being is. Any animal who wishes to communicate with you has something to share with you!

Ninety-nine plus percent of animals stay in remembrance of their soul purpose throughout their incarnation. Few forget. When they do, it is the response to neglect or abuse and can be changed as an animal recovers and heals. However, even most of those who have been hurt remain alert in this way. So when you ask an animal to share his or her soul purpose you are asking a highly validating and respectful question. You are asking: "Who are you?" You are suggesting you care to know. To most animals, this feels like a loving invitation.

Animals will proceed to let you in on why they incarnated. Purposes may range from supporting a person, creating peace, being in balance, having fun, being joy, learning patience, shining light, nurturing, developing an answer to a cultural need, sharing with other animals, helping a child to have confidence, being a parent, and simply being, to a vast list of other missions and focuses.

C. Self-Doubt

Self-doubt is a beautiful and natural way of keeping oneself in check. It is a naturally occurring mechanism by which you will remind yourself not to project onto another. It occurs for everyone in practicing animal communication. When self-doubt arises, there are a variety of ways to address it.

First of all, remember that each animal is distinctly unique, as is each human. Your key to answering the question: "Am I receiving this animal or am I making stuff up?" will be in identifying the uniqueness of the mode in which an animal is speaking to you. If every animal you speak with talks in the same way, you are focused more on *your* individual self than the individual self of the animal. If each animal's communication is distinct, you are very likely receiving each particular animal's communication. Each animal you speak with will be different in his or her communication modes. Some will use particular words that are not words common in your own vocabulary. Some will use sounds. Some will carry feelings that are unfamiliar to you. Some will have distinct and memorable voices. Each animal will be like a particular flavor that no other matches.

Simultaneously, it is important that you not take this recognition to an extreme. Your conversations with anyone—animal or person—will be a combination of you and them merging in some way. Don't expect yourself to disappear fully. Something of who you are, what you value, and which aspects of life you naturally gravitate to will be reflected in the conversation. Simply expect yourself to behold each animal in a way that has a unique flavor.

Another way to address self-doubt is to ask the animal with whom you are conversing to provide clues as to the accuracy of your perception. Animals have intelligence and talent for finding ways to do this. Some animals use eye contact, others send strong feeling toward you, and others may find playful or humorous ways. Stay alert and trust that animals will find a way to let you know. Many animals send thoughts right into your own brain so that you will have a re-occurring thought. Some animals are masters at creating communications made perfectly for the person they are aiming to reach.

Now a seasoned holistic vet, Dr. Stephen Blake shares his initial insecurities when beginning to use homeopathy, acupuncture, and flower essences with animals (*The Pet Whisperer: Stories About My Friends, the Animals*, 2003) One of his first clients, Brandy the dog, gave him a purposeful and well-meaning, reaffirming lick to encourage Dr. Blake onward during a moment of doubt. Brandy was accurate as Dr. Blake's judgment proved itself true by healing Brandy.

When I first began to fully hear the animals, I had self-doubt and asked for signs to indicate I was not just imagining. During a walk with my significant other, Ray, I met a lizard with whom I conversed. The lizard scampered up my leg and torso, placing himself on my back to join us for a twenty-minute walk. When Ray and I went to the Hawaiian island of Molokai for the first time, I was greeted by a dog, named Charcoal Beauty, and two splendid kitties. They escorted me to the beach. In that moment I had an impulsive idea. I called from my heart across the sea, "Whales; if you are truly communicating to me all these months as I believed, offer a sign!" At that moment a big whale jumped out of the water, landed back in, and splashed it's giant tail up and down for half an hour.

In an article called "Animal Communicators and the Hot-Cold Game" (2009) by Janet Roper, Janet says on the issue of self-doubt:

> To my thinking, one of the basic guidelines of animal communication is trusting what you receive. It helps to think that of all the trillion and 2 thoughts, feelings and impressions in the world, that one came to me at that specific time from that specific animal.
>
> It's about trusting that we interpret the information from the animal as the animal intended us to, but even more than that, it's about trusting ourselves! About trusting ourselves so much that we don't feel the urge to have the information verified from another source.
>
> Times have changed, and we are now being asked to rely on our own guidance and inner knowledge. The animals are great

teachers to us in learning this lesson, and many animals are ready to aid us. See: http://EzineArticles.com/3068302.

I will always remember the time when I received information from an animal who was lost and yet I asked my client to call someone else because I was not a specialist in missing animals. I did not trust myself to extend my abilities into this territory. I had been told of another woman who was an expert at working with missing animals and sent my client her way, explaining I would share what I heard but did not specialize in the topic. The client called back several days later to say that everything I had told him was correct, wheras the information relayed to him by the specialist was off the wall and bore no resemblance to what proved true.

Still feeling uncertain on the topic of lost animals, I referred another client to Annette Betcher who had helped me years ago when Jessie was missing. Prior to Jessie's reincarnation and my animal communication awakening, Annette had assisted me. A true specialist in lost animals, Annette was secure enough to help me overcome my own insecurities. Instead of taking over, she surprisingly encouraged me to trust myself, and I thank her to this day. I felt that she behaved as many an animal would, eager to support my own self-worth so that I too could be of benefit to more animals. The varied experiences contributed to my own self-trust. The universe has a way of providing what we need as we learn and grow in self-trust.

A woman named Cindy Young had intuitive conversations with her animals but doubted herself so she called an animal communicator in California named Teresa Wagner. Teresa told her all kinds of accuracies about her animals' feelings, relationships with her, relationships with each other, and her dog Grace's past. What Teresa told her mirrored her own unspoken feelings, thoughts, and intuitions so completely that she came to trust her own abilities. Cindy shares her experience with Teresa in an article titled "Grace's Story – Part II" published at www.animalsinourhearts.com. There is no formula for how we come to trust in ourselves but there is endless help available as we reach out and stay open to receive.

In a humble and personal sharing called *Exploring the Levels of Creation (2007)*, Sylvia Browne, a well-known USA/American psychic often featured on Larry King, discusses error. She says that all intuitives will make errors as to err is to be human. Even the best of intuitives who are mostly accurate will make mistakes. This is true in all professions, so being willing to be wrong, apologize, and go on, is a needed trait for an animal communicator who practices professionally

Amelia Kinkade, in her book The *Language of Miracles* (2006), discusses a long encounter she has with a person whose dog is missing. Uninvited, yet caring and generous, Amelia replies to the poster about a lost dog, offering her services pro bono. Through many conversations with many disappointing starts, the dog is at last located. Amelia deciphers that the false starts, which were very challenging for the person involved, may have been alleviated if Amelia had asked the dog different questions in the beginning. The dog's final communications to Amelia tell her this is so. With great humility, Amelia utilizes this dog's offering to her, as a teaching to bring to future appointments. In the face of a mistake, assume that you are hitting your learning curve. Even masters of a skill will be faced with new learning curves, new lessons, and reminders of humility throughout their practice.

D. Continuing the Conversation

Acknowledge each animal for sharing with you by thanking him or her once your conversation has begun. You may now ask whatever questions you have to ask. Then you can practice listening. The better you become at listening as an empathetic witness, the clearer your communication will become. Remember to validate all of your animal's experiences.

You may also ask the animal what s/he would like to share. I have spoken with animals who can sum it up in about five seconds and others who have gone on for an hour or more! Like personalities, there are unlimited animal-ities to behold. Animals will have many kinds of focuses, as do people. Topics from spiritual to emotional to mental to physical to very practical are all discussed. Animals have much to offer to the world of ecology, spirituality, religion, medicine, science, art, global peace, philosophy, politics, and psychology, so remain open to these beings. You may be surprised at all you find out.

E. Finding Your Innate Intuitive Abilities

Animal communicators tend to agree that everyone has innate intuitive abilities. A person's ability to communicate with animals stems from the degree to which that person is able to honor his or her intuitive capabilities as real. Everyone has ways in which he or she is naturally intuitive, i.e. telepathic. Everyone will access these abilities to greater degrees as they validate them and use them. When you use a brain muscle or a physical muscle its strength grows. When you use an intuitive muscle its strength grows.

Because all of life radiates energy and all of life receives energy, telepathy is actually very rational and practical. For example, if a person or a bird is thinking of her home, s/he radiates a visual of her/his home. If a cat or a lion is experiencing joy, s/he radiates the vibration of joy. If a dolphin or a whale is experiencing the frequency of lights, colors, and tones of bliss, s/he radiates the lights, colors, tones, and bliss. If a goat is thinking, "I love you," inside his or her head, the words vibrate in his/her entire heart and body then out into the world.

Pictures, words, sounds, emotional feelings, physical sensations, and scents vibrate. As a person begins to surrender into his or her own heart, eventually it is understood that everything on the outside is actually inside. We have immediate "internet" access with everyone and everything everywhere in our own hearts! Animals accept this, and thus telepathic heart-to-heart communication is a natural state for them. As humans have become conditioned over millenniums to devalue, dismiss, or paranormalize telepathy, re-focusing on telepathy, with thanks, will allow it to blossom in a natural way. Utilizing telepathy within oneself will assist it to grow in a way unique to each person. Nature can take care of this.

As signals are sent out, we all have the capacities to receive them. If you look at an email, you see the email and you receive the message. If you look at the images someone is sending you receive the images. If you feel the emotions of people in a movie as you watch, you are receiving their realities. In the same way, you can receive feelings that are not being spoken about via the feelings in your own body. You can see pictures radiated by another. You can hear thoughts of others. It is all inside you. Studies show that the vocal chords of everyone in an audience at a concert begin to vibrate like the singer once the singer sings. All of us can begin to reflect that upon which we focus. As we focus on a person or animal, who they are can begin to move through our own being. Based on our own make up, we will see, feel, or hear the vibrations of others to greater or lesser degrees.

To access your own intuitive abilities, notice the ways in which you have always been intuitive. Do you get a feeling when a friend is about to call? Have you heard thoughts of others at times? Have you seen images that give you information about an environment? Have you met someone and had an immediate feeling about who that person is or the effect they may have on you if you invite them into your life? Perhaps your intuition has alerted you in ways unique to you. Begin to validate this and pay attention to it. This is the doorway into your individual way of being telepathic.

In addition, you can realistically suspect that the regular senses you most rely upon in day-to-day life will be similar to the ones you use with your intuition.

For example, if you are very focused on what you see, you are likely to be more of a visual intuitive. If you are very alive with what you feel, you are likely to be a feeling intuitive. If you are very alert to sound and music, you are likely to be an auditory intuitive. If you are centralized in your physical sensations, you are likely to have the key to experiencing the sensations of others. This extends to inspired feelings and scents as well. All communications, telepathic or not, are vibration. So, in a sense, what we have learned to call regular sensory perception is a kind of telepathy. It is the result of reception of vibration, as is what we call telepathy.

Aim to notice when you block off intuition, dismissing it as imagination or turning away from receiving it. This is common and a great blessing to notice. Once you are aware of tendencies to block intuition, you can choose to stay present and see where your intuition leads you. Everyone has unique gifts with intuition. In the same way that every therapist and healer has a unique understanding of their clients, every animal intuitive will have a talent that reflects his or her life focus. Some are better skilled with understanding the comfort needs of animals. Some are better skilled with understanding the emotional needs of animals. Some are more gifted with hearing the spiritual experiences of animals. Some are medical intuitives. Each one who communicates with animals will find that she or he has more energy around a particular aspect of communication than other aspects. This is similar to any kind of conversation between people. Some like to study philosophy while others like to fix cars. What you have studied in your own existence is what you will most naturally pick up on in the world of another.

F. Synchronicity

A woman was meeting many animals who were dealing with issues of unworthiness. She began to wonder if she was projecting her own issues onto the animals. As she inquired more deeply into this with the animals she found that she was really attracting animals who shared her issue. In this way, she and the animals were working on healing the issue together. It can be expected that you will attract what you need. Like attracts like.

When I was an intern therapist at the University of Vermont, many of my clients were suffering from the loss of a parent recently passed over. During an interns' group-supervision meeting, I mentioned that the secretary was interviewing the clients and sending them to the right counselor. Another intern who had recovered from alcoholism confirmed that almost all her clients were struggling with alcohol recovery.

"How does the secretary know all the confidential information from the clients' intakes?" I asked our supervisor. "I thought that information was off limits."

"She doesn't," the supervisor explained. As our group inquired more deeply into this, we found it was commonly shared. We realized it was synchronicity at play, which is related to "the law of attraction" as recently popularized in *The Secret* by Rhonda Byrne (DVD; 2006). The law of attraction is a mind focused on what it wishes to see manifest. Synchronicity is surrender into what is occurring and the magnetic creativity of the universe that naturally brings beings into the same mode of experiencing to one another. Animals are aware of this principle and allow its impulses to assist them in development during an incarnation.

As my own training continued via life itself, I realized that this type of synchronicity is ongoing. We attract what we are metamorphosizing through and in this we can all help one another just by being ourselves. If a variety of your animal friends are going through passages that reflect something in you, you can understand that this is natural.

For deeper understanding of the law of attraction and synchronicities involved with being our natural ourselves, please read **Success Love Now** and **Healing and Awakening the Heart. I published both of these books in 2013**

drawing upon a decade of focused work with my cat Jessie and other animals on these matters.

On a public web forum on synchronicity, someone posted that the red-tailed hawk shows up in his life frequently.

"It was about 3 AM Saturday night when I was reading and looked back over this particular author's take on the significance of the red-tailed hawk. Well, Sunday afternoon I stepped out onto my deck to enjoy the crisp air and to my utter amazement I looked up to see movement from my roof only to catch the red-tailed hawk leaping from the roof right over my bedroom and flying off. Talk about validation, he had been perched right above my bed where I'd been reading and meditating on hawk just the night before."

The synchronicity of animals we meet, how we meet, when we meet, and why we meet is experienced by people from all walks of life.

Kim McElroy, an Equine Artist (www.spiritofhorse.com), writes that the process of each painting involves unplanned synchronicity with animal meetings and human meetings. A painting she creates to reflect a human seeing oneself in the eye of a horse cracks. In an effort to keep the crack from damaging the painting, she looks for something to put over the crack. Her friend had given her an owl feather that was left when an owl died on her friend's property, so Kim adds an owl feather to the painting. Soon, a woman meets Kim, sees the painting, and feels it was made for her. (Kim has found that every horse painting she makes is being created specifically for someone, often a person she has yet to meet. The animal's magic is always at sacred play.)

Kim feels she must tell the woman about the owl feather and the crack before selling her the painting. The woman explains that the owl feather, a symbol of death and transformation, represents the death of her son. The crack is an American Indian tradition. So as not to think we can ever be God, it is customary to place a crack in a painting as a symbol of our flaws. The woman who purchases the painting knows it is for her. Her husband and son were native Americans. Kim was open to receive and guidance took her.

Kim also shares of geese who loved her Mother and appeared in her life on behalf of her Mother who has passed. The world of animal synchronicity will bring us new truths, great nourishment, and Divine nectar when we remain open. This can only occur via a soul and heart that are listening and a mind that assists the heart and soul.

G. Stay Open to Others' Differences

Although you will rely upon the sensory talents you are given more than anything else, you will benefit animals and yourself by staying very open to the unfamiliar. Let's say you are a very word-oriented person and you are speaking to a snake. Perhaps this particular snake is more attentive to the physical in his or her personal orientation. S/he sends sensation through your skin as a way of sharing his or her world. You may feel uneasy at first, out of your territory, unsure of how to respond. Of course, this can happen between you and another person just as easily. People from different cultures can quickly misperceive one another if time is not taken to receive another deeply, hear through another's ears, and feel through their hands. So choose to stay present and be aware of the world of someone else. To know another means to be in his or her skin for a moment. If you stay present, you will adjust.

Another example of this is an emotionally oriented person speaking to an intellectually oriented animal. Perhaps your day is full of feeling. You talk to a cat who is very mentally oriented. At first you have trouble keeping up, as you might have also experienced with very intellectual humans. But stay focused and you will begin to glimpse inside another's life.

Animals who are shaman/shawoman and master teachers will inspire new feelings in you. You will find yourself literally breathed into great joy, love, peace, silence, serenity, abundance, compassion, and heart opening beyond anything previously experienced. As you open to this, not only will you know their worlds, but you will reach new territory inside of you. Eventually you will awaken to the place where you are one with all. Many of the animals are adept at bringing you there. Some communicators believe that all animals who come into a person's life are teachers, guides, and shaman/shawoman. I interpret this as follows: Every being on the planet can bring some kind of transformative power to each other being when they meet. The universe has a way of bringing those whom we need to meet, for their benefit and ours, into our lives. As animals are, in general, awakened, we can learn lessons of awakening from all animals in our connecting with them.

When Jessie and I began our relationship he brought me a bird. At that time I was not hearing Jessie although I was feeling him. I missed the point, brought the bird into the bathroom, closed the door, and called an animal rescue place for help. Jessie had curled up by my heart after kissing my nose every night from day one. We slept soundly and magically together. After my display of upset with the bird, Jessie moved outside to sleep on a little cushioned chair at night. I learned from animal communicator Gina Palmer that I had hurt his feelings by rejecting his wedding ring. The bird was meant to symbolize our union. It was his way of saying I will stay with you forever.

Once I understood, I apologized profusely. Immediately I was given a squirrel. I thanked Jessie over and over, rejoicing and celebrating the wedding gift. Jessie moved back into my arms at night. In every occurrence between person and animal, a gift is available. Under every action is a special communication or learning to unfold. Whether preferable and desired, or seemingly problematic communication, both hold a message of love.

H. Rituals with Emotional Value

Animals have evolved individual and group ways of interfacing with emotional passages in healthy ways. If you have not been included in a group ritual among animals assume it is because they have yet to take you fully into their world. As you respect in an innocent and reverent manner, an invitation to watch or even participate is more likely. Many people have not witnessed animals' rituals, parties, and sacred events because they have not become close enough to animals as equals.

One day at the Hidden Valley Sanctuary I was invited to watch a group of deer play circle tag out on the field. All the deer stood in a circle. The deer who was the tagger would run up to another. Next, both stood facing one another on hind legs as the tag took place. The one who was tagged would then become tagger. The entire event took place in a circle. I asked them to share about their own experience of the event.

Here was the answer from one of the elder females: "We are family in wind and in fun breeze. We share our game to let you see that games can be developed to take us deeper into our spiritual knowing. Our oneness and our unseen magic into other realms existing beyond physical and accessed within physical is the basis of this game. We have unique personalities but in essence we come from one and our ritual leads us (and you) to this. We want to share with you that games may exist without the win/lose paradigm that people often enjoy on your planet."

In *Animals in Spirit* by Penelope Smith (2008), a staff member at an elephant park was granted permission from a tribe of elephants to bear witness to their grieving ritual. The night before one of their members died, the group participated in a vocal and physical mourning and goodbye ritual, allowing deep emotion to be expressed.

Available to view on YouTube is a film about Anna Breytenbach (https://www.youtube.com/watch?v=gvwHHMEDdT0) showing her tender and understanding relationship with animals of the wild. Animals of the wild befriend her calmly and lovingly as she offers full understanding to them. Inviting us into her heart-born relationship with wild animal friends who previously respond to humans with depression or anger, Anna shows us what we missed. When embraced with empathy, respect and love, these animals respond in a new way.

Echo of the Elephants, was a PBS/BBC special that documented anthropologist Cynthia Moss who has lived by elephants for twenty-five years. Able to get closer and closer to the elephants as time progressed, she was allowed to witness a sacred sexual ritual. The elephants revealed that their mating practice is done in a group. A female will mate once a year. When she mates with a male, the entire tribe surrounds them and merges energetically, adding sound and vibration. Everyone is spiritually transformed via this sacred event. An elephant reported when asked, "We cry light and sound of awe and power to the Heavens. We pray for protection from any danger when the new one being created today is born. We base our feet to our Earth, we sing in pride for this is the beginning of a new being to come. This being's life and energy waves are initiated through this first beginning."

Little Creatures Who Run the World, a film directed by Nick Upton (1998) reveals ants to be a highly sophisticated society. While human beings have been on Earth for one million years, ants have been here for thirty million years, The total of all body weight from all ants on our planet is equal to the total body weight of all humans. Dr. Edward O. Wilson from Harvard University, who has studied ants all over the world, believes that their longevity is due to their tribal setup. Each ant has a specific job that benefits the entire species. Even if the job will end the ant's life short, the ant willingly gives her or his all for the betterment of the society. Male ants who mate with the queen will die afterwards but do so any way. Sisters may die in their work but that does not stop them. All for one is the game. I watched a group of sisters who were on a path to get food. They stopped to touch each other any time one met another on the trail. There were hundreds so there was a lot of stopping and touching going on. Chemically they were giving each other communications on location of food. "Emotionally" one of the sisters commented, "I am tenderly stopping to love my sister." There are new babies being born all the time and other ants dying all the time as they work together so the communal family can go on for millions of years! Many told me they reincarnated numerous times back into the same family.

I interviewed an ant about their way of life. She said, "Our purpose is the big light. My individuality shines through my work in all ways necessary so there is no need to focus on it. I focus on the big light. There are souls here who have experienced being other species and were very eager to have this experience in which the one light is the shared focus." I noticed that the ant I spoke to was living in music and a beat generated by self and those in the shared society, much like a group chant. Life here and now was the reality. Keen individual intelligence specifically directed and also shared by a merged group mind was present. I felt the ant's great awareness of her entire community as herself with her individuality to be at the center of her own reality experience.

Hawks and ravens at Hidden Valley Sanctuary called me with a quack once a day. (One of the ravens quacked as ravens are capable of learning the sounds of other bird species.) This meant that I was to come outside. At that time I would be circled and messages were sent to me and/or a client on the other end of the phone if I came out holding the cordless while in session. When I asked them why they chose to work with me in this way they said, "You opened your heart and asked us." This was true.

Animals will devise ritual in fun ways, also. Many years ago I lived with a boyfriend and his cat Max. Max and I loved to play ball. One day, when I wasn't looking, Max took his ball and placed it in my sneaker, which was in an open suitcase. He lodged it in where I would not see it right away. I had half packed as I was getting ready to leave. Later, when I opened my suitcase in another town I found the ball and laughed wholeheartedly. Max said, "Remember me! Remember Me!" with some joy and also some parting sorrow. His personal ritual was helpful to us both. His fun style elicited joy with our union and brought forth a conscious allowing of the missing feelings as well.

We all know of cats who take us into their lion-pride and mark us as territory with a cuddly hug and kiss. Rubbing their foreheads and mouths on our skin or clothes, cats are acknowledging our importance to them while scenting us with their glands!

At the time during which a very gifted and serviceful teacher, Yohinta, the black cat with a golden mark on her forehead, was getting ready to pass, her animal family created ritual (Penelope Smith, *Animals in Spirit*, 2008). Sherman the feline brought gophers and rabbits and also cuddled Yohinta. Sherman, with Belinda and Buddha Boy, two canines in the family, marched around their home sanctuary land with her. It was her desire to give gratitude to the land she loved during her last hour. The process was very consciously created by all members involved. We need not underestimate the wisdom and intelligence of animals. Their emotional lives are as rich as the emotional lives of humans. They live from the eternal, beholding the individual as an expression of the infinite. Humans may learn from animals on this matter.

Many humans live as the individual in the physical/personality world longing to re-find the eternal. Many animal communicators discover that what has been missing and yearned for is re-found as they learn to be like animals. It was Dove Jonah who took me to my first remembrance of the neutral void happiness out of which all is created. Jonah has stayed with me ever since. He did his work with me via a little ritual. He climbed all over my body and, perching himself on my shoulder, whispered in my ear, "It's easy."

I. Speaking with Animals Passed Over

Telepathic animal communication with animals who have left the body is practiced precisely in the same manner as with animals in body. Animals remain able to see, hear, and feel all of your communications when they pass. Often they will connect with you in ways that help you to recall the eternal realms. Animals are at peace with passing. Sometimes they will hold your emotion for you until you are ready to be in peace yourself.

People have many deep feelings when a beloved animal passes. It is important to honor all of these feelings by allowing them to pass through your body in their own natural cycle. As you open to them they open you to greater love.

It is vital that you complete all your communications with your animal friend on the other side. Make sure to thank them, ask for forgiveness, apologize if there is a need, and bring into the open anything else that comes up. This will allow you to transition through your own emotional layers of completion. You will be more open to reuniting with your animal friend from the unconditional soul place this way. This is most healthy when we transition from one form to another in any relationship. The formula remains the same. Send gratitude, send questions, and send all communications from your heart to their's. If you need validation that your animal friend is experiencing your communication, ask. S/he will find the right way for you to receive this affirmation and build faith. Transition is offered as a time of great deepening for all involved. In the biological experience of all emotions that accompany what is indeed ephemeral, we dissolve deeper into our remembering of what is eternal. In this is great love.

Take into account that your animal friend most often spends his or her life attempting to turn you on to the unconditional realms. S/he works like a magician to help you re-find yourself here. Once she or he has passed over it becomes harder for him or her to relate through the conditional realms and illusional realms. So, see if you can tune into that which is beyond circumstance, i.e. the state of being peace, joy, love, gratitude, kindness, abundance, and compassion to fully appreciate the entirety of the message that your animal friend will wish to impart from the other side.

Penelope Smith includes the experiences of many animal communicators who have translated for animals on the other side, in her book *Animals in Spirit* (2008). Recorded in this book, is the true account of a woman named Annette. Annette calls animal communicator, Jacquelyn Smith, about the sudden loss of her beloved cat Karl who dies of a stroke during a teeth cleaning. Through Jacquelyn, Karl is able to mention topics sacred and known only to Annette, thus confirming Annette's knowing that it is truly Karl speaking. He tells her "just as a tree bears fruit, we will spring forth again bearing fruit. We will be together again. I leave you with the image of a multifaceted diamond which reflects the light in all aspects."

In Annette's own words about his communication, "this pierced my heart." Annette had buried Max with a diamond earring of hers between his paws. The communication helped Annette to cry with grief for her loss and simultaneous ecstasy for her union with her beloved in spirit.

It was my beloved cat Jessie's speaking to me from the other side that taught me the reality of unconditional joy. In between incarnations he told me that the magnetism of our joy, which had brought us together initially, would naturally bring him back to Earth. He shared that he remained in joy of our love with or without a body. In this loving gesture, he showed me that my joy was not circumstantial but innate and available within me at any time. Once I received Jessie's gift wisdom as my own, he returned to me in a new physical form. He came back to live with me in another cat body.

Often clients come to me with unresolved grief from an animal who has passed anywhere between an hour and many decades ago. Once they are able to receive word from their animal, learn the animal has remained close, share their grief, and complete any dangling concerns, a sense of great relief comes. Return of fulfillment is available. Until communication is made, a sense of separateness and incompletion can stay stuck in the waves of consciousness of the heart.

I will always remember a woman who had been in conflict for thirty years over the death of her cat, carrying guilt because she had to leave this cat with another person. When she discovered the cat had continued to love her, adore her, and only remember her with gratitude for all she had given, she dropped a long-term load and found a new inner freedom. This touched me and relieved the guilt I had carried for leaving my beloved childhood cat Tiger-Lily with my brother, sister, and parents, assuming this was best for her when I went to college. Years later I realized I did not talk to her to allow her to make her own choice. Many audience members who viewed our interaction during a public Satsang were also cleansed. Animals teach in a mysterious web of many who are reached in their passages. They call us home to completion when we leave dangling emotional threads.

In an interview with Gina Palmer, a delightful animal communication teacher who encouraged me to notice my innate animal communication abilities, I learned of her communication with Charles IV. Charles is one of her family members and a friend of mine who is a dachshund. Via ongoing communication, Charles assisted his family with letting go and re-finding him when his time came to die and be reborn came about.

Charles was the Father of a big animal family of cats, rabbits, birds, and dogs (about thirty all together). Charles took on the head of the family role and attended to everyone's needs as an unconditionally giving father. He even filled in as a substitute Mother of nursing for Sno, a sweet and profound temple Goddess Kitty who had been weaned too early.

Charles' death came on suddenly when he took on the energy of another distressed animal who came to visit. Within twenty-four hours he had passed. Staying in close contact with Charles, Gina was able to appreciate Charles' consciously made choice.

As much as he had loved being the Father figure, he had fulfilled the role completely. He now wanted to move on and experience being an inner child for the duration of his next life. He felt that leaving by helping another and making a quick exit was a good way. Soon he would come home as a child. He gave Gina directions on where to locate him.

In a short time Charles was back as another dachshund who was very different in color and size. The animals recognized him immediately for animals look at the soul first. Cinnamon, another dachshund family member, ran to Charles and said, "Brother, oh brother!" Home again but with a new mission, Charles was embraced by his loved ones. The animal family knew who he was regardless of form. By staying in contact, the grieving process was largely fulfilled for Gina and she was ready to reunite in a new way.

Animals who are existing on the other side are ambassadors for us to access what we most need within. Because the outer signs of sound, visual appearance, and soft fur are missed, animals' bodiless presences are not readily available to everyone. A great longing occurs when the physical form is left. When we follow this longing into the deepest chambers of the heart, we find our animals are still there. The help of an animal communicator who can serve as a liaison, until the human is ready to do this for his/herself, is a great asset. There are now hundreds of accomplished and highly gifted animal communicators all over the world who are able to help. Animal communicators can work by phone because animals can talk long distance and from the other side. *Species Link,* a quarterly Animal Communication magazine that is designed by Penelope Smith, features the writings of many communicators. Listed in every issue are hundreds of animal communicators from around the world who you may contact for assistance.

J. Counter Transference or Duality Reality

Counter transference is the act of placing our own agendas onto another, and seeing them largely in terms of our own reality creations instead of their own. The reality of duality includes an element of our seeing ourselves in others. How we see everyone else is colored and shaped by our own reality. Understanding another requires us to see, for a moment, through their own point of view. This is the beauty and gift of living on a planet of many beings. The ongoing attentiveness an animal communicator requires is an awareness of both of these potential aspects of communicating: counter transference and duality reality. The animal communicator will benefit animals by noticing that whatever the communicator perceives has a focal lens originating in how s/he perceives life in general. From this witnessing of self, the animal communicator must check in to make sure that he or she is hearing an animal in terms of the animals' own viewpoint rather than through a judgment.

An example of a human entering into counter transference occurred with a horse. This woman was sure that a horse was upset with her. The horse explained that he was in unconditional appreciation of her. Simultaneously, her pushing away an aspect of herself (dislike) was energetically affecting his body so as to feel repelled (this would be the case if she did this with a human, too). His taking space from her furthered her belief that he was upset for emotional reasons that she would help him heal. When finally she dropped this counter transference of diagnosing him and settled into her heart, her analysis of this horse vanished. In this moment the horse felt at ease with her and approached her openly.

Animals are enlightened and able to be. If we understand them through concepts of better/worse or what our minds believe should be in place of what is, we may be overlooking the reality of their focus. There is a reality of being fully present with what is experienced by the animal with whom one is conversing. This dialogue is heart based. This conversation comes from entering another's consciousness through experience and neutral witnessing rather than judgment or analysis.

Within this reality, disharmonies of the mental and physical and emotional can be addressed. "Addressing disharmonies," as Shera the cat explained, "is a matter of retuning. Tuning out- of-tune instruments ready to be retuned is different than fixing something wrong. We don't fix problems because we know peace in everything. We simply retune out of harmony music." To understand animal worlds, speak within this concept instead of the fix-what-is-wrong ideology.

Duality reality means that you have a unique focus this incarnation based upon your own life purpose. Therefore, you will see life through this lens. You will attract beings who will have their own reason for merging in some way with your world. By being aware of your purpose and lens, you will remain respectful of the artistry and subjective aspect of all communications.

A woman called me about her goat on the other side. When I spoke to the soul who had once been a goat I was surprised as he seemed as much human as goat. He stood next to me on two legs and offered wisdom. I experience him to be very similar to Jesus. I have met many masters among the animals who remind me of great teachers like Gangaji, Ammachi, Buddha, Ramana Anandamayi Ma, and others. Although I arranged the session to serve a woman, Amy, and her goat, Jonathon, it was obvious to me that Jonathon was coming to me as healer. He approached me and filled me with deep inner peace, taking away everything else. He offered me comfort.

When I told Amy, she explained that this was just like Jonathon. He was a healer, teacher, and great loving force of light during his embodied life and afterwards. As he rode a wheelchair this might account for his two-legged appearance. Jonathon told me that he had also been human in another lifetime, another reason for his appearance. (Many animal communicators report animals telling them about past lives as humans. However, many animals also report being an animal over and over or even one species over and over. An animal may choose to be one species repeatedly due to a love, attraction, and joy with the particular species experience.). Amy confirmed that she always felt him to be human. Amy went on to say that he had taught her of care and love in a very profound and purposeful way. These two, with a soul contract that could not be denied, were two master teachers of love.

I asked Jonathon what his intents had been with Amy. He said, "I came to give her back her light...to have her see herself again in full."

"Did you also benefit as a learner?" I asked. I realized this brought a bit of shame up for him. I recognized this shame to be my own as well. In facing it, the shame vanished. Suddenly and simultaneously, we were both converted from powerful teachers to tender children in need of a sweet and soft cry, a release of emotions from the body. We comforted one another. Amy's energy was at once present, taking on both roles as well.

"Yes, I needed to know I could both hold myself fully as spirit and receive help," he said, "so I took on a body with a disability."

You can see that Amy, Jonathon, and I were each benefiting in ways we each needed, within this arrangement of relationships in which all three of us were communicators, healers, and the one being healed. There only was one. The teacher and the teaching were all of us. After I wrote this, Jonathan nuzzled me on the face as a Goat in Spirit and said "I have returned in goat body."

Gina Palmer, author of *Paws & Claws Newsletter* (2001–2006) took readers through her personal adventures with beloved animal family members. Any challenge that occurred revealed a gem inside, created both for Gina, via her experience, and her readers vicariously. To teach the gift of complete liberation, love, gratitude, and peace in all situations, a dove named Jonah was born. Healthy and sweet, he came in with a song of love. Soon after his birth he was unfortunately attacked by a bird who was asked to leave the sanctuary due to his hostile behaviors. Little Jonah survived with abrasions and blindness. Gina took little Jonah under her wing, created a condo for him, and kept him attended to all day. He escorted her wherever she went. With love and wonderful attention he learned to fly, play, and live as the beautiful soul he was. His only messages were of love and gratitude.

Jonah was one to bow in reverence to everyone and everything he met. He is the little bird who, along with Jessie Justin Joy, was the catalyst for my re-emergence into a whole new way of being. Eager to bring others into an infinite truth I encountered from my bird and cat facilitators, I began to teach in a new way. Soon I met a spiritual teacher named Gangaji who defined what I was sharing as "awakened consciousness." I had to credit Jonah and Jessie. Jonah is an awakened teacher who comes into lives of people when needed. In following Gina's journeys, the synchronicity of how and when animals appear in a human's life shines brightly. What could be called coincidence is shown to be the grand ability of universal consciousness to bring beings together in right way, right place, and right time!

Chapter 2

Animals as Shaman/Shawoman, Teachers, and Guides

A. Divine Teachers

Just about every animal communicator who has written books on telepathic animal communication has come to find that animals operate as shaman, shawoman, teachers, and guides. Animals find ways to open human hearts and minds back to states of unconditional qualities. Animals take us out of the conditioned and into the inspired. While many Gurus told me that peace was the state of being here and now it was a little dove, named Jonah, who was able to get the message through my every cell. While many spiritual teachers told me that joy came from within it was my cat, Jessie, who delivered this awareness so deeply into my being that it became my own.

A woman was terribly sad because her dog had passed over. This dog said she would be returning. The woman felt it to be so but was despondent because the reunion had not yet occurred. She consulted me to find out if it was true and when it would happen. Her dog expressed that her return date could not happen until the woman, Connie, returned to peace.

Connie lived two hours from my home. Several months later she found peace within and had an intuition to visit an animal shelter near my home instead of near hers. She did not tell me about this and was not sure of why she was going to drive two hours instead of going to a shelter near her. Something inside her told her to do this.

On the day she came to the animal shelter near my home, I had an intuition to visit the same animal shelter and give them some guest passes to my seminars. We arrived within five minutes of each other and were delightedly surprised to find one another there. We were introduced to a dog. Angels appeared. One soul left a canine body while the soul of her beloved dog entered the body. Connie and her beloved companion went home elated and so did I. We had been ushered not only into unconditional peace but into trust in the Divine's ability to provide great grace and to answer prayers with fulfillment.

There is a learning that can occur only when we do not know what to expect yet remain open. Animal communicators attest to the fact that learning of a spiritual nature takes place in surprise and not knowing. Usually in the great love a person feels for an animal, the heart is given over to something greater than control. The heart is given over to something beyond what the mind first thought to be truth so that a discovery of the unconditional realms is found.

Jackie Geyer *(Animals as Teachers and Healers*, Susan Chernak McElroy, 1997) shares about one of her teachers, a sweet female raccoon who ate dinner at Jackie's home each night. Jackie watched her raccoon buddy find some food in the trash bins outside her office window each night. Jackie became quite fond of this friend who happened to be missing one leg. One time, Jackie witnessed her little friend show up with one of her three legs severely injured. Jackie burst into great tears feeling the unfairness of what this one had to endure. Jackie gazed in amazement as this one hoisted her body into the air, took several steps on two front legs, rested, and repeated the process over and over.

Many months later, Jackie's raccoon friend did not return for two weeks and Jackie was very sad, assuming another accident had occurred. Then, to Jackie's astonishment, her raccoon companion came back, leg healed and three little ones with her. After that Jackie felt gratitude for her life in place of areas in which she complained previously. This one was her teacher and role model. Animals find very non-invasive yet poignant ways to share and express themselves for our benefit.

In her book, *Animal Talk: Interspecies Telepathic Communication* (2008), Penelope Smith discusses a humpback whale named Humphrey who made the worldwide news. Humphrey crossed under the Golden Gate Bridge, through San

Francisco Bay, and up the Sacramento River to what could have been his predicted end. People tried many methods to get him to turn around, assuming he was disoriented. He eventually returned to the open ocean. When Penelope contacted him she learned that he was purposefully making this journey to help expand the consciousness of humans. Chosen as a purposeful emissary by a group of whales, he agreed to make this trip, even if he were to die, in order to move humans. His plan was to reach many people so that they would become more aware of their effects on the Earth, the seas, the whales, and all life on Earth. Often, upon speaking to animals who seem to not know what they are doing, a bigger purpose that is selfless and generous is revealed. Although it is always our responsibility to assist animals in need, it behooves us to find out their purpose before operating as helpers to them.

Carol Raymond, in *Animals as Teachers and Healers by* Susan Chernak McElroy, tells of an incident in which she was full of worry—her husband said that his new job required them to move. In the midst of her fear, she prayed. Soon a deer came to the window, looked into her eyes for a long time, and purposefully delivered her into unconditional peace. I have seen a similar occurrence between a deer and a client who lived in our neighborhood, when I was giving a session.

The client was distraught and asked for help. A deer stared into her eyes from outside the window for many minutes until she found renewed faith and courage.

B. Whales

Whales are now suspected to have life spans of 200 years or more despite previous beliefs that their lifespans were shorter. In a personal interview, Captain Veto (a.k.a. Robert Veterino), a marine mammal naturalist who has spent his days among the wild dolphins and whales of Big Island Hawaii for a couple of decades, cites evidence of whales genius, intelligence, and longevity.

Whales are often called the record keepers of all time, able to store historical memory in a brain with a size that none other can match. Many people have experienced movement into states of oneness, deep devotion, and manifestation abilities as well as altered states into multidimensional paradigms in the presence of these sacred beings. Like wild dolphins, wild whales will converse with humans when they choose. Dolphins and whales cannot be chased and will, by far, outswim any human. Meetings are created on the dolphins' and whales' terms. These terms tend to be gentle-hearted and loving. Dolphins and whales will approach the openhearted and go out of their way to acknowledge people with flips, twirls, close eye contact, songs, kisses, and other glorious presentations and initiations. They will transport humans into new realms of comprehension and experience.

"We live in a deeper level of reality than most of the life forms on Earth, and we understand the larger picture. We are masters of expanded states of awareness, which include more complex dimensions beyond your own. Within these realms, we see sub-atomic particles as part of a greater whole, which is holographic and indivisible. We are involved in examining multiform pictures that we create and that are also created by you. We understand how these pictures create reality on Earth," was channeled by whales to Joan Ocean (*Lightstream* Magazine, 2006).

I interviewed Captain Douglas Webster who has spent over a decade swimming and speaking with whales and dolphins in Kealakekua Bay, Hawaii. He is a very playful chap, full of laughter and great respect for the cetaceans. He knows them to be fully conscious and intelligent beings. In an article posted at www.dolphinville.com (originally published in *Lightstream* Magazine, 2003), he states:

"The dolphins and whales know more than we do!

"Yes, that's right. After millions and millions years of evolution, these biological entities have developed sentience and forms of intelligence that reach far beyond our limited linear processing and intellectualized reality paradigms.

"The Cetacean species, which includes all whales, dolphins, and porpoises, have evolved sensory apparatus that makes even our most sophisticated instruments look like tinker-toys by comparison. For millions of millennia they have had free reign on our water planet—an abundance of food, and no predators for the most part. Their primary activities consist of playing, eating, and copulating. Not bad, eh?

"Think about it for a minute. Our aquatic cousins have lived in perfect harmony and balance for eons of time. Maybe we can learn something from them. The fact of the matter is we know next to nothing about this sublime species of mammal that chose to move back into the ocean nearly fifty million years ago."

Some of my initial experiences as oneness, after Jonah the dove and Jessie the feline opened the door for me, were with the whales. In the whales' consciousness a complete knowing oneself as all that is becomes reality. This is an exquisite peace. Joan Ocean describes being with whales as: "I relax into the silence. I become aware of a huge all-encompassing cloud of blissful emptiness. Allowing it in, I am lost. There is no me. There are no thoughts, no body, no ocean, no Joan. I am emerged in a state of sublime peace that defies definition." (*Dolphins into the Future*, 1997).

While each animal species has an ability to coax, nudge, guide, and invite humans back to their true nature of unconditional peace, love, and oneness, the whales will communicate only in this way. To communicate with a whale is to remember the state of the eternal, to dissolve back into essential essence.

C. Dolphins

Dolphins have become well known for approaching humans with unconditional love and invitations into other dimensional experiences of bliss, joy color, sound, and wordless ecstasy. Well known for their ability to immediately take humans into high frequency experiences of indefinable happiness and unconditional love, they are highly intelligent and deeply embedded in the here now present.

Speaking to Trish Regan about her experiences with dolphins and whales, I learned how unconditionally loving this human dolphin guide and spiritual teacher is. She credits this to dolphins and whales. She tells a story in her two book series, *Essential Joy: Finding It, Keeping It, Sharing It* (2002), of being in a very graced state of love from her dolphin friends who surrounded her and invited her in their pod. Out at sea, she ran into an irate person who was convinced that Trish was hurting the dolphins. Faced with the raving, ranting, and inability of this person to hear anything, Trish found her self to stay in love. She could see the love beneath the fear in this person as the dolphins have done with so many people. The person was relentless but Trish could only stay in the love, and at last, this person surrendered to the love, also.

I spoke to Celeste Eaton who has been swimming with the dolphins in Kealakekua Bay of Big Island Hawaii for many years. She shares that the love they bring is gentle and kind. At her website www.celestialsonics.com, where she shares a variety of her dolphin encounters, Celeste writes:

"It was a beautiful morning as we ventured out again to see the whales. We got into the water where it was very shallow. Only 20 feet below me was a mom and calf lying on the bottom. I was lying still above them when they started to come up. She began to lift her peck fin, turned, and saw I was too close, looked me in the eye and brought her fin back down beside her, making sure she didn't hit me. She sent me the most loving and gentle look of nurturing, then moved on with her calf. That night I couldn't sleep and was told to write the message from Aqualaw (she was overseeing the whales). Here is the message as I transcribed it:

'We are to move past what the physical eyes can see into the greater reality, the expansion into Oneness. You were shown this by seeing and feeling the mother whale today and into her expansiveness and then to the Stars expansiveness, especially Sirius. She's saying there is no difference above and below...expand yourself to encompass both realities simultaneously, then we are both and all at the same time, there is no space or time between the two accept what we perceive as separate. Move from a state of separateness to Oneness or Wholeness of Being.' "

I interviewed approximately twenty people who swim with the dolphins on a regular basis about their experiences. Everyone concurred. The dolphins take people into playful bliss and happiness beyond cause. Allowing all emotions to be found in joy and all experiences to be found in ecstasy, they offer colors, healings, and a love that is profound. To go into the dolphin world is to find an entirely new type of existence.

Trish Regan, Douglas Webster, Robert Veterino, Celeste Eaton, Joan Ocean, and Meg Sibley, all dolphin guides, moved to Kealakekua Bay on Big Island, Hawaii specifically to be with dolphins and whales. Each felt called to come experience and teach in some way—so much so that they left jobs, homes, and lives to start fresh with no guarantees—simply a profound love calling. Each of these teachers, having now been in Hawaii between four and twenty-five years, report zero regrets; only great fulfillment. After arriving, Meg Sibley founded a dream institute she had planned for a long time called Dolphin Sound. In her book, *Dolphin Notes: Insights from My First Summer with the Dolphins,* she credits these beings for bringing her into states of receptivity, patience, and heart connection. She attributes qualities of joy, peace, and delight to the dolphins with whom she swims regularly.

D. Individuality and Species-ality

As is the case with every person, each animal is a unique individual. Each being has a completely original set of focuses, intentions, characteristics on the mental, physical, emotional, and spiritual plane all packed into one art piece of themselves! Don't assume anything. Simply ask and witness and experience to learn the world of another!

Each species also shares some similarities. Each species has a unique energy form and way about them. Each species has a wisdom specialty just like each individual does. For example, canines are protectors who carry a very present earth now tone while cats are swirly magicians who tend to remain half here and half on the other side. As you spend more and more time with a species you will encounter the uniqueness of each member as well as an overall similarity in style. You are likely to absorb their magic and truths. You may realize that their sacred energies have been inside you all along and they are your stewards, taking you back to all you are meant to be.

Like a person, an animal may tend more toward a physical nature, an emotional nature, or a spiritual nature. Like a person, an animal may have his or her central energy focal point located in a particular chakra. Like a person, each animal will have a distinctly unique and non-reproducible set of physical, mental, emotional, and spiritual characteristics that make them who they are.

To know an animal, stay openminded and openhearted at all times. Like people, animals go through growth, change, and transformation during life experience. An animal is an ever-moving life form of soul married to body-mind-personality for a particular incarnation.

E. Reincarnation as Initiation

Animals take people into deep transformations as they reincarnate or speak of future possibilities. Forever bringing in their shaman/shawoman abilities to teach and guide, they are loyal assistants to their people. An animal often knows if she or he is to reincarnate before s/he leaves.

Animals often know when they will leave. One woman called to ask if she should euthanize her dog. Her dog said, "No, I have more lessons for you but when we are complete I will die in your arms." A few days later when this woman had found peace, her beloved died in her arms.

Years later he said, "I remain walking with you in peace as spirit. Some day, when we are ready I will come again in body to take you home where you long to be. Again we will walk; you as learner and me as both physical follower and inner guide. For now our work is complete until you are ready to take the next plunge. I am by your side in spirit, forever your animal."

One dog, named Cisco, said, "Yellow flowers will grow in the yard after I leave." At this point my human client, Cheryl, fully doubted what I was saying as she had no yellow flowers. After her beloved Cisco passed, yellow flowers grew once a year in her back yard. There is a magic and a knowing that animals have with their comings and goings. Cisco came back temporarily and visits from time to time by sharing a body with Cheryl's current canine companion, Lucky. As both canines are very warm and loving, the body share is a compatible way for Cisco to stay off Earth for a while, something he needs for his own peace and nourishment, This arrangement also allows him to make physical visits for the enjoyment of both Cheryl and himself.

Reincarnation is forever a teacher. Each person who experiences the return of their beloved animal, with the animal making his or her re-appearance crystal clear by personality quirks and clues or soul energy, shares this. The lessons are different for each participant in this *leela*, a Hindu concept meaning The divine play in which we perceive ourselves to live our lives. . The lessons are consistently messengers of a divine unconditional experience in love.

Sonya Fitzpatrick relays the following occurrence in her book, *Cat Talk* (2003). Samuel was a loved family member. As a dog he shared his life with a human couple, Keith and Frances, and two cats, Belinda and Spike. When he passed, it was devastating for his human family members. Distraught with the loss, they decided not to get another dog.

A short period later, a scruffy tabby in need of food appeared at Keith's work place. Keith fed him. The next day, the little one came to brush affectionately on Keith's leg. Keith decided to take him home. Keith and Frances watched in amazement as the little guy was greeted by Belinda and Spike who sniffed him from head to toe and acted as though he was already family. As the kitty walked through the house examining each room, Belinda and Spike followed him. When the kitten woke Keith up one morning, as Samuel had done, by gently nibbling Keith's' ear lobe, Keith realized that Samuel was back! Consciously chosen departure, purposefully presented flowers, ear nibbling, and a multitude of other signs can bring about recognition and trust in a familiar friend's wisdom and re-appearance. In these moments, an even deeper telepathy takes place, assisting the person to fully realize that their loved one is back (or capable of making such a choice in the future). People who have experienced reincarnated animals return (or animals consciously choosing how to leave the body with messages of potential later return) report the experience of an overwhelming love. The telepathic transmission that accompanies outer signs erases all doubt.

While it may take a little bit of time for a person to notice his/her animal companion has returned in new form, animals notice right away. This is because animals see all beings as souls and witness personality and body to be a temporary costume like some clothes. In the same book that describes Samuel's reincarnation, *Cat Talk* (2003) by Sonya Fitzpatrick, another reincarnation excursion is shared. Margaux, a dog, brings attention to a little kitten so that his person notices him. Margaux's person, Marcia, whose cat Leonard had recently passed, decides to take the kitten home to her other cats. When they arrive, the new kitten, now called Hennessey, takes over Leonard's litter box, walks like Leonard, and opens the cabinet with his little paws just like Leonard did. Champion, one of Leonard's playmates, runs to Hennessey and kisses him as though he is family. This is when Marcia realizes why Margaux had taken such interest in Hennessey. Leonard has reincarnated as Hennessey and re-found his family.

People frequently ask me how they will find their animals if their animals reincarnate. The answer is always the same. Your animal will find the way to you. The animal will orchestrate a situation in which you will find each other. Signs will be given to alert you. Animals are capable of re-seeding their souls in bodies that they feel and believe to be conducive to their soul purpose as well as your own. Time and time again, those who study animal communication find that animals' communication abilities are far more advanced than human ones.

Chapter 3

Animals as Caretakers

One night Ray and I were visiting two human friends. Their cat, Dez, walked out into the living room as it got late and told her human mother that it was her mother's bedtime. Dez also made sure that her mother's energies were in balance, attending to her as a thoughtful feline energy worker. Animals who incarnate to attend to the wellbeing of a specific person or another animal will do this with steadfast devotion. A darling bird who I met when I was invited to give a Satsang in Crescent City, CA, kept tabs on everyone throughout the event, She made very appropriate verbal remarks to assist, including sounds of jubilation when someone was triumphant. When it was veering near my time to go, she said for the first time in the entire two days. "It's about time to go."

In Stephen Blake's book, *The Pet Whisperer: Stories About My Friends, the Animals* (2003), Stephen discusses a feline client who was caretaker during his person's pregnancy. Sheri, the human workaholic, would be meowed at repeatedly until she took time to lie down and rest. As she rested, her kitty, Mr. T, would lay on Sheri's stomach for hours, tending to the developing baby. When their little girl was born, Mr. T was at the door ready to greet her upon her arrival home from the hospital. He escorted the family right into the nursery.

In the book, *The Compassion of Animals: True Stories of Animal Courage and Kindness,* by Kristin von Kreisler, the true story of a gentle pig living in Houston with her human loved ones is described. This pig was docile and played with her family's human children in the day, sleeping in a pile of leaves at night. Raised from a piglet into a 300 pound adult, she was a member of the family. One unexpected day, robbers approached the neighborhood. This pig showed another part of herself at this time. In order to protect her human family, she threw the robber to the ground, kicked and bit him, and pinned him there, not letting him go until police arrived.

In Sonya Fitzpatrick's book, *Cat Talk: The Secrets of Communicating with Your Cat* (2003), Sonya shares the story of her beloved goose, Primrose, who had a short life with Sonya when she was a child. Sonya was born with an innately developed talent of conversing with animals. She shut this gift down after finding her friend, Primrose, and several other geese family members slaughtered for dinners. She spent her early adult years in another field. Thirty years later, Primrose reincarnated as Wellington the Cat, purposefully reminding Sonya of her ability to speak to the animals. With Wellington's return, Sonya, revived her conversations with animals and established her career as The Pet Psychic.

Wellington stayed with her for twenty-one years this time, died in older age, and then reincarnated again as a feline in her life.

In *Animal Voices: Telepathic Communication in the Web of Life* by Dawn Bauman Brunke (2002), Dawn interviews a midwife llama in a tribe. The llama is very dedicated to assisting mothers with the entry of their newborns into society. She considers this to be her job and also trains younger llamas for the same job. During an interview with Captain Douglas Webster, who has been swimming with dolphin pods and whales for over a decade (www.dolphinville.com), I learned that the whales' mothers sometimes have an auntie assisting with the child raising. Animals who come to be in caretaking roles for humans, and/or other animals, tend to take their missions very seriously and lovingly.

I told the coyote that I met at the Hidden Valley Sanctuary that Jessie was my son and to please respect this. She said she would. She also asked that I respect her family and come to understand that she also loved her young and was protective. She wanted humans to understand that she was just like us and to drop any bad images of coyotes as only being predators. I sent her and her family much love and respect from then on. A family member used to walk into our driveway and we never had any trouble.

In *Animals in Spirit* by Penelope Smith (2008) a true story is shared of a coyote who was asked by an elderly cat, Oscar, to help him leave his body. The coyote made sure to contact the cat's person, Sue Hopple, an animal communicator, by approaching her three times and even limping like the cat, Oscar, to get Sue's attention. Oscar had told Sue that he would be leaving soon and had purposely gone to the coyote. The coyote left Oscar's body for other animals to eat and explained, "I could have taken any of your cats any time but never did. I have watched over you. I was an Indian in my last life. I only took Oscar's body because he asked me to help him go. I helped and am leaving the food for others."

Susan Chernak McElroy shares the story of a little comforting dog who came to her in a time of great need (*Animals as Teachers and Healers, 1998*). The evening before her seventeen-year-old son's unexpected and tragic death in a diving accident, Susan noticed a tiny red dog at the cemetery, seemingly waiting for someone, as she drove by. The next day at her son's funeral, the dog was there during Susan's overwhelming grief. The following day when Susan returned to the grave sight, right by a mound of flowers at the grave was the little red dog again. Seeing Susan, this tiny one stepped back in respect. Once Susan sat, she came closer and asked for nothing with a presence suggesting, "I am here just for you."

Susan asked her, "Are you alright?" and she wagged her tail.

"Are you my guardian angel?" Susan continued, and the dog looked deep into her eyes and soul. Susan remembered Callie, a little red dog her son had rescued from an arrow injury and had taken in until the day she died. After a few more days with the dog at the cemetery, Susan took the little one home.

When she asked her canine friend, "Are you Callie?" the dog wagged her tail furiously, ran to Susan and placed her paw on Susan's knee. Callie's returning reincarnated, with the intention to care for son passed and Mother alive, was kind and evident.

Coming to the planet as a caretaker can occur in a variety of ways. An animal from any species may come with this role. We know when animals are here as caretakers by their actions and the energy encompassed in these actions.

Chapter 4

Animals as Messengers

I was called in by a local computer agency because a staff member had killed himself unexpectedly. A therapist was needed. Although I had never met the man or his family, I agreed to lead a grief circle the next day. Late, the night before the grief circle, I sat in the living room at the Hidden Valley Sanctuary, wondering about this man. It was then that I heard a knock. Who on Earth would be knocking this late at night, I wondered. Also, it was not coming from the front door. What was going on? The knocking persisted. I realized it was at the window. I looked and there was a beetle knocking. When she saw me she stopped.

The beetle came to tell me of the person's death and to be a liaison between us, which prepared me for the next day. I came to understand his regrets, his feelings, his love, and his desires. Via the beetle, he came to feel safe with me and chose to attend the grief circle I led, helping me to do so. Nobody in the circle mentioned seeing his presence but he was felt by many.

My next encounter with a beetle was with Lucy at a house we rented in Los Gatos for a year. She would knock for me and then fly into my office when I answered the door. She liked to listen to me play guitar and was often found in the bed with Ray, Jessie, and me when we rose in the morning. When it was time to leave that house, she left too, leaving her shell right by our bed. The movers cleared everything but somehow missed the shell so I found it. She tells me she orchestrated that for peace. She dehydrated her body and her soul flew on.

I missed Lucy and a year later, in our new sanctuary home, there was a knock. "Lucy is back," Ray called out. Lucy had flown in, circled Ray dramatically and landed in front of him. When I ran out she flew to me, landed on my body and stayed with me for many hours. This time she came to teach me faith and trust in the Divine intelligence and the care surrounding my life. I put her (actually him this time) on a tiny blanket by our bed on the dresser. In the middle of the night, I woke up to find Jessie and Lucy (now Luciano or Luc) playing tag, running up and down the hall. When Luc saw me, he came and landed at my feet, and so did Jessie. Luc really wanted to sleep with us in the bed and flew onto it. I was concerned for his safety so I asked him to sleep outside and return later on. His shell was a beautiful mosaic as it had been in her first life with us.

Again, I did not see Luc for many months and one day called out with my heart, "Luc, where are ye?"

At this time Luc was not incarnated so a grandchild was sent. I found the grandchild (same mosaic shell that Lucy and Luc had worn) waiting for me at the door the next day. He sat with me and then flew to the very top of a tall tree. This time I was given the message of faith in life, ability to accomplish through surrender, and divine guidance. I was told not to give up during a time when I was beginning to wonder if my missionary planetary visions in full form would ever come true!

In the book *Cat Miracles* (2003) by Brad Steiger and Sherry Hansen Steiger, the true account is told of a cat who was able to teach his family of his psychic powers. Kitty-Kat was able to relay messages of his needs to the family, whether they were awake or asleep. If he needed to be let in while they were asleep, he would speak to them via dreams. He was even able to ring the doorbell. One of his human family members, Reverend Bob Short, was unsure if Kitty-Kat was able to use mind-over-matter to ring the bell or if he actually jumped up and pushed the doorbell. Either way, his messages were clear!

Animal Miracles: Inspirational and Heroic True Stories (1999), another book by the Steigers, gives word of a horse, Old Gray, who broke the barn down and charged out. Running so fast that her human friend named Ray had to get in a truck to keep up, Old Gray seemed to have a passion and a mission. It turned out that Gray had run to the scene of a fire where she dragged her human friend Jeremy out, and brought Ray to find him in time to save his life. Otherwise he would have died. Old Gray knew that Jeremy was in trouble, knew where he was, and knew how to get Ray's attention so that Jeremy would not be left alone.

Although we have been taught to think that human awareness, intelligence and wisdom surpasses animal awareness, intelligence and wisdom, we might look again. Animals are privy to occurrences that are beyond many peoples' capacity to comprehend if we are not located in the sensory circumstances of their happening. Story after story of animals who found their way to new homes when people moved, crossing hundreds of miles, while facing seemingly insurmountable challenges have been documented in the Steigers' books.

Perhaps the key to a healthy world in which ecology, politics, and psychology are one, and serve everyone, is available. Is it possible that we can have a globe that leaves no person or being of any species void of love, food, shelter, and clean water? With the advanced knowledge of many animal species, this may be possible. Consider turning to the animals for answers in the areas in which humans have caused great destruction for self and need. New guidance, holy perspectives, practical astuteness, and a broad picture of circling past, present and future circumstances are available by dialoguing with animals and accepting their wisdom.

As I write this, a big white bird has come in Spirit with a message, flashing light in my office. "There is a simple way and humans have much to learn. We are here to help. Call out to us and we will answer through your hearts, through our animal forms, and additionally in many surprising ways for the benefit of all of you. We will help but you must allow us. Breathe us in. We are your familiars, your ancestors, and guides. We are here. Please do not be lost. Please work together with us. We can keep you from harm, alert you to your beauty, and show you the way to a kind, gentle, and non-conditional style of living in ease. Please take our guidance."

Chapter 5

Animals as Rescuers

One time when I was on a lone hike deep into the Hawaii forest I came across a solitary man. For reasons of intuition only, a chill went through me. While Hawaii is known as a Paradise, it is also known for rape and crime that goes untried and unchallenged with an ineffective police department. Scared, unable to hide as the man was near me and he saw me, far from other humans or animals, I was precarious. Immediately, two beautiful big dogs appeared from nowhere. They ran to me as though we had always been together forever, greeting me as their own. Each one escorted me close, one on each side all the way back to town, about forty minutes. When we arrived, I called their person from the phone number on their collars. He was shocked and could not figure out how they ended up so far from home. He said he would have to drive quite a ways to get them and came in a truck to pick them up. They said, "We felt the joy in your spirit moving all through the forest and we were afraid you could get hurt. We were asked to escort you by your Mother from the spirit world and some angels in the spirit world, too. We were told to find and meet you and we were given the right timing. Thank you for receiving us."

Brad Steiger and Sherry Hansen Steiger have collated a variety of true stories from people who have been helped by animal heroes. Humans whose lives have been saved by a bird, shark, cats, and dogs are mentioned, among others. A teenage girl came home to a two-hundred pound, six-foot tall stranger, who started to grab her, when her one-pound bird flew in and attacked him with beak and claws until he ran out crying and whining. A family tipped their canoe out at sea in the dark and was approached by a shark who alternated between circling them to ensure their safety, lightly touching each of them to let them know he was safe, and swimming slightly ahead of them, guiding them back home. They were great swimmers but had lost sight of where the shore was so he guided them back and stayed near until each one was out of the water. Cats woke up their human family to save them from fire and a dog led his person home for two hours when he was lost, after protecting him from a potential incident with three rattlesnakes. The dog chased his person away from rocks upon which he was about to step because the dog sensed the rattlers behind the rocks where the person did not. The dog turned out to be accurate. The person was spared from stepping on rattlers and potentially being bitten.

Animals are highly alert and conscious beings, aware through many senses, when sometimes humans are not. They will go to great measures to help. Stories like these are not uncommon. Allen and Linda Anderson and Marty Becker have collected a variety of writings of situations from people who experienced animals as angels. Included in this book, called *Angel Animals: Divine Messengers of Miracles* (2007), is Linda Lansdell's portrayal of her work. She brought rescued animals to children in group homes. The purpose was to have people and animals, who felt thrown away by society, heal together. She vividly recalls a time when a rabbit, victimized cruelly by being dipped in oil, came to the children barely able to breathe. These kids, often detached or insensitively tough, became loving and tender in the face of the rabbit's condition, reaching out to help, providing genuine care. The rabbit and the children revived each other.

Animals are privy to others' experiences because they utilize telepathic communication. Animals receive pictures, feelings, and thoughts from people, situations, and places. A dog can learn about another dog's ancestors and current life with a sniff. The vibration of another dog's experiences travels through scent. Selfless loyalty is not uncommon for animals.

As people learn the language of animals, people become more of the universal heart and more telepathic, which go hand in hand. In this process, it is common for great feelings of awe, devotion, and reverence to take over.

Chapter 6

Animals as Advisors

After receiving information from an animal communicator (also called an animal intuitive), a person may decide to seek wisdom from particular animal family members or friends on a regular basis. After learning to dialogue with animals, the same is true. A very common story is one of a single person in pursuit of a human mate. His or her animal companion will make strong statements about a potential mate who visits the house. While a "not right" statement about a date can be misinterpreted as jealousy, it is often a deep recognition of who will bring happiness and who will bring trouble to an animal's human beloved. Animals who tend to be patient, calm, and respectful will go as far as attacking, biting, or even pooping on the belongings of a person if they sense their beloved human is in threat. In the same spirit, animals will kiss, cuddle, and make a big welcome notice of someone who is inwardly kind and brings the right love.

It is important to ask an animal to clarify their message. A message of the kind indicated above can be anything from, "not the right one for you" to "you are in serious threat." An animal will do their best to relay the message to you. When a potential mate is a good soul, but not right for you, it can be a complex task to let you know. For this reason, learning to dialogue with an animal who is a good advisor for you is valuable.

Advice about a potential mate is only one example of advice animals may offer. Wisdom extends into all life categories. As is true with people, each animal has particular domains of interest and expertise. The ways in which different animals are able to advise is endless. When an animal is born to be an advisor, it is important that she/he live out his/her potential. Just like a human being, an animal who is satisfied in life is fulfilling his or her purpose, utilizing his/her talent, and being acknowledged for his/her gifts of service to others. The more you understand your animal beloved's gift, the more your animal feels loved and understood. The more you are able to utilize your animal's gift to you, the happier you both feel.

Chapter 7

Animals as Buddhas

Animals are very clear on their essential purposes. Each being has an essential purpose that is very simple and can be summed up in a word or two. As we awaken into higher and higher states of consciousness, we find our purpose to be more one of being than doing or having. A purpose that is based on being, naturally includes doing and having in related ways.

An animal may experience his or her purpose to be peace or to be content or to be joy or to be love. The list of qualities of being is long, including all inspired states. Quite often, a person with an animal who is born to be a particular quality has both a yearning to be the same quality and an ability to be the same quality. Your animal can remind you of how to dissolve into a state of being. In focusing on his/her vibration, you find you are more and more like your animal friend.

More and more, people are being graced to receive the enlightened teachings of their animal friends. Magic Cat, who is the companion of humans Yael and Doug Powell, candidly exposes his views on awakened life. Magic Cat invites us to say "yes" to love with his insights into the web of life, sacred sexuality, our minds, death, and hunting practices, among other topics. Magic Cat's main premise is to be present in this moment. Yael is able to hear Magic Cat, so she has recorded his book, *Magic Cat (an enlightened animal) Explains Creation* (2004).

Chapter 8

Animals as Mentors to People and Animals

Animals take on mentoring roles with other animals as well as with people. Shera, a medicine woman feline who lived at Paws and Claws sanctuary was Sno's (feline) mentor. With help from animal communicator Gina Palmer and a holistic veterinarian, Dr. Stephen Blake, Shera healed herself of several life threatening diseases including cancer. Shera explained that everyone and everything is made of vibration. An out of tune vibration is experienced to be what humans call illness and a tuned vibration is what humans call wellness.

Shera (now named Babyra in her current incarnation), who lived well into elder years, was one to teach via osmosis and verbal guidance. One time, when I was feeling extremely sick to my stomach, Shera appeared long distance. She instructed me to feel fully into my belly beyond any description of what I thought was happening. She encouraged me to go fully into the sensation beyond any verbal explanation. Once I surrendered fully into the sensation, sickness ceased to be problematic. My resistance to pain left and the lack of tuning in my belly simply was. In this, I found I was fully free in pleasure, in pain, and in neither. I watched old conditionings and feelings pour out of my belly energetically and then the illness was gone.

Jessie Justin Joy took in a student named Buster. Buster was a little kitten who liked to jump in our cat door and follow Jessie everywhere. If Jessie slept, Buster slept. If Jessie played, Buster played. Buster was enamored of Jessie. I asked Jessie about what he was teaching Buster. "To think Big," Jessie said.

I asked Buster what he liked about his time with Jessie. "He was all there and he was a Father to me who understood my language and guided me well on principles and matters of the world," was Buster's reply.

In J. Allen Boone's book *Kinship with All Life* (1954), Allen blatantly reports that the dog he was hired to train was really there to train him. When an animal comes to be a mentor to a human, she/he will make it clear. Whether the person is as perceptive as Boone and able to acknowledge this or not, an animal who comes to mentor can find ways to do so.

Chapter 9

Animals Not Honored

Animals, like people, have needs on every level. In the same way that spiritual teachers are often misperceived as being ones who are supposed to be needless, so are animals misperceived. An awakened and enlightened being of any species has needs on every level. Being witness to these needs, rather than glued in attachment to these needs, is a different energy form but does not negate needs.

One time, a donkey and a sheep lived together on a small plot of land with a family. They spent their days in love and communion with one another. So blessed was their personal relationship that they felt as one with two personalities. Without consent, the humans decided to give the sheep away. The donkey bellowed in huge cries all day for months for the entire neighborhood to hear. It would not have taken an expert communicator to figure out what was going on and to have behaved honorably toward the donkey and sheep. Unfortunately, these two were regarded as less important to the humans who came to the conclusion that the sheep would be better off on a bigger farm without asking the sheep.

Years later, the donkey and the sheep have learned to communicate from afar but the donkey feels betrayed, angry, and sad. The sheep has found an easier time adjusting.

It is advisable to ask your animal about his or her needs on every level: emotional, physical, spiritual, mental, and anything else. To give someone else a life that meets their happiness is a great service. A human who has an animal as part of his/her family has this opportunity.

I have heard people say that "pets" have it easy. They get fed and are not required to work. I find this to be lacking in understanding of animals who live as family members with humans. Every animal I meet, who lives among humans, has taken a devotional task of some sort to heart, mind, and body. Animals tend to do so with great regard and unconditional attentiveness to people. They are known to work around the clock, as needed on behalf of humans, in a profound and dedicated way.

Chapter 10

Animals Honored

Animals who are honored will respond in many ways. As mentioned earlier, JoJo the dolphin would even go fishing for Dean Bernal. He trusted Dean enough to let Dean administer antibiotics when JoJo was hurt. Although JoJo was known to be missing from a particular beach for months at a time, he consistently reappeared within minutes, any time Dean came back to the island.

Animals who are treated with love, respect, and care will reveal more and more of themselves, as is true of humans. As I write this book, I have been approached telepathically by snakes who are teaching me that they have intricate dances and customs that create energetic fields for all of life on the planet. They are masters of vibration in the same way that sitar musicians learn to master the effect they have on vibration in consciousness.

In the 1980s, I informally interviewed a student of Ravi Shankar named Roop Verma. Roop, who is globally recognized for his concerts, is the musical author of *Harmonie* (2009), among many other pieces of music. I learned that Roop spent four hours a day on one note for many days in his musical studies. In eastern music, this means he spent time on four notes for every two notes we use in the West. This intricate relationship between sound and human is the basis for manifesting creations in conscious harmony. He learned to be the note, know the note, express the note, and create the note in unison with life. He learned different patterns of music designed for the creation and bringing about of states of consciousness in humanity.

Snakes, though poorly represented in the human world, tell me that they also work in this way. While I have been writing this book, a snake has appeared near my feet by my path. Others have contacted me via visions, vibrations, and dreams. I ran into a woman in an airport in Loreto, Mexico who was able to film the unique and exquisite spiral dance of two snakes mating, something rarely seen. The magic and awareness of sound, patterns, and math in the snake world displays exceptional intelligence.

Any animal species you approach can speak to you about vibration. Each species utilizes their relationship between self and sound in conscious ways. Some animals are able to hear the notes that emanate from trees, people, and each other. Animals are secret magicians and Saints with powers used for the good of many. Dolphins are beginning to get the credit they deserve in humanity's eyes for their vibrational understanding and master artistry. The more that humanity gives credit where credit is due, the more we will be invited to discover, experience, and witness the intelligence that animals have to share. As we make ourselves available by honoring our sisters and brothers in the other species forms, we will be given mentorships in love. Each species offers something unique, as does each individual animal.

When a person is having problems with an animal, the person is likely to be having problems with his or herself. The animal's call for a person's attention via behavior reflects a disharmony, a question, or pregnant gift getting ready to come out of the person's consciousness with the instrumental gift of the animal. Many people report new depths of compassion, talent, love, joy, abundance, and ability when responding to an animal's call that is communicated via behavior.

When I received the visit of a snake in reverence, I was taken into self fully. Deeper than the void of love and joy I knew as home. I was a non-existence of nothing in relationship to nothing. This non-existence situation was deeper than peace itself. All vibrations have a math, a color, a sound, and an effect in the world of inspired emotion. When disregarded, all vibrations have biological emotion. In the center of this is absolutely nothing. Animals are conscious of this while they live their lives of duality simultaneously. Animals who are honored will guide you into your own awareness.

A man I chatted with in the grocery store shared that squirrels and hawks visited him, sat close to him, and waved to him because he respected their intelligence.

The animals are masters of the yoga of nothing and everything, yin and yang, creation and dissolution. They know the unattached world and within this they know great love and creative power. Honored animals will guide you into ancient teachings in ways that speak to you as a unique soul of consciousness. The logical mind, trying to understand, will miss the vacancy in which stillness is everlasting and movement is forever available for good. Your opportunity is be open to your animal friends and family members. You might meditate with your animal friends to learn firsthand what they have to impart via heart and soul. Like master teachers' gifts, what animals can teach you goes deeper than language. Language may be a starting point, however, to take you there.

In *The Language of Miracles: A Celebrated Psychic Teaches You to Talk to Animals* (2006), Amelia Kinkade tells the story of an orangutan named Julian who is ill. None of the doctors in Julian's abode know what is wrong and none of the doctors speak to animals. One of the veterinarian technicians, Darren was a student of Amelia's who did hear the animals. Julian turned to Darren and said "Tell the doctor I have pneumonia."

Darren immediately asked the doctor if she had considered the possibility that Julian might have pneumonia. The doctor replied that Julian didn't have the symptoms for pneumonia. A few days later tests revealed that Julian did have pneumonia. The orangutan knew all along, well before the staff did. He also knew which person on the staff would be able to understand. The one who honored animals to be coherent, capable, and self-knowing was the one to whom the orangutan turned and spoke.

A dog named Faith was born with only three legs and one had to be amputated. The vet suggested putting her to sleep. But her person, Jude, as well as Jude's children, loved Faith and they became family. Faith, the dog, was assisted by Jude to learn to walk on two legs. She now lives a full life and is even a TV star. She is a very angelic being with a clear heart of gold who makes many people happy. She teaches perseverance. With love, miracles can happen.

Chapter 11

Animal Emotions

The embrace that Christian the lion gives to his human friends, John Rendall and Ace Bourke, upon reunion (www.oprah.com/media/20090313-tows-christian-lion), will erase the doubts from anyone who questions animals' deep capacity to feel. Christian runs to his human friends after a year apart, embraces them passionately, and next, introduces them to his lioness wife. The lion trainer who took Christian onto his land told John and Ace that Christian would no longer remember them if they came to visit. John and Ace had found Christian at a department store, living trapped and unfairly. They bought him, took him home, cared for him, walked him in the local church grounds of grass and loved him. They became family. When he became too big to live in the city they sought out a new home for him. In his new African home, Christian and the lion he married live among his lion pride. The notion that animals forget people is a misinformed notion. Animals remember their loved ones eternally as evidenced in this heart-opening video. This is universally true.

Animals feel emotions just like people do. Elephants weep. Cats grieve. Birds rejoice. Snakes fall in love.

All species feel all emotions. There are two types of emotions: biological and inspired. In the realm of unconditional awareness, biological feelings become waves within inspired states.

JoJo the dolphin was very protective when he met his life mate and pushed his best friend Dean away from her. He felt jealous of Dean. His bliss state could hold the jealousy as a biological wave within an inspired state.

When Sno the feline lost Charles the canine, she sat on his grave with her arm stretched out for four days.

Many animals are known to run around in great joy a few minutes before their people arrive home after work. They can feel their people coming and they rejoice. I have heard this story from a variety of people.

The spectrum of emotions on the planet is vast. It is part of the experience of all species—human and animal.

Chapter 12

Insects

J. Allen Boone in his book, *Kinship with All Life* (1954), shares his adventures with a fly who comes to him as a teacher. Insects can be communicated with in exactly the same way that animals can.

I had a friend spider named Jason~Jasona who lived with us at the Hidden Valley Sanctuary. I used to spend time with Jason~Jasona on the stairwell every afternoon. When our landlord made a sudden choice to sell the property and we had to relocate, I told Jason~Jasona we were moving. The next day Jason~Jasona hung herself on her spider's web.

When I spoke to her about her departure, she said, "I am still weaving webs in the light. I left my form as we have to part but I will find you again." She flashed me a picture of a golden web ladder which she spun, climbed upon, and fulfilled her devotion to life through creating. She appeared as light herself.

Several years later I was meditating in our new sanctuary in the same chair every morning. Every day Jason~Jasona, now in a new form, meditated on the ceiling directly above my chair. Some days she would purposely drop a little spun blanket (spider size) into my hands as a gift. I saved one. When I hold it I am filled with a vibration of golden fulfillment.

Insects are intelligent, communicative, and full individuals just as people are. You will learn to interact with them by using everything you practice in telepathic communication with animals.

Chapter 13

Life of the body Ending

Penelope Smith relays an interaction she had with a rabbit in her book *Animals in Spirit: Our Faithful Companions' Transition to the Afterlife* (2008). The rabbit lived at a rabbit farm. Penelope asked the rabbit if she was upset about living her life on a rabbit farm. The rabbit said that she liked the accommodations, the beautiful farm, the free range, and the food. She was very happy with her life. Penelope asked, "Aren't you upset that you will be eaten?"

The rabbit explained that everybody is eaten. Even people who are buried in the ground are eaten by the Earth itself. The rabbit said the purpose of life is to enjoy oneself while we are here.

In Dawn Baumann Brunke's book *Animal Voices: Telepathic Communication in the Web of Life* (2002), Dawn interviews cats on the topic of predator and prey. A cat explains that Mother's teach them to hunt when they are young. The first rule of hunting is to ask the prey if (s)he is ready to go and desiring to go. If the animal who will give his or her body to be eaten says "yes," then the hunt is done in honor. Often the prey animal will jump out of the body so that the game of the hunt is not one that causes ongoing pain. An animal can leave a body in an instant.

Often, when an animal is ready to go, she or he will find another animal to assist. The two are friends and simply help each other in this way. A wonderful chicken who lives at Paws and Claws Sanctuary, who received a $3000 operation to prolong her life when she had more life to live, at last decided it was time to go. She asked a coyote to come take her in the night. I learned of this in an interview with Gina Palmer, the author of *Paws & Claws Newsletter* (2001–2006).

As told in *Animals in Spirit: Our Faithful Companions' Transition to the Afterlife* (Penelope Smith, 2008), a cat who had completed her life asked a dog to help her leave her body. The dog, who was not in any way antagonistic toward the cat, obliged. The dog said he only felt love for the cat and was doing what she asked.

Because animals experience themselves as souls wearing costumes (i.e. body-personalities), coming and leaving is not seen as tragic. When an animal is forced to go before she/he is ready, as in the case of undesired euthanasia, this is tragic. When animals are mistreated in factory farms this is tragic. When animals are honored in life and death they speak of it all as well and good. It is important to include and honor animals in all choices of life-and-death details and plans.

When a person believes that euthanasia may be best, that person will be in service to the animal by asking the animal if this is the animal's desire. Many an animal knows how and when she or he is to die. Sometimes animals will be in very challenging physical states but will choose to stay for the sake of a loved person who is completing a lesson. Sometimes an animal will be ready to go and will choose to exit his or her body on his or her own. Sometimes she or he will request euthanasia. Always ask. Each animal has a voice, a purpose, preferences, and good reasons for his/her decisions.

If you talk to a few vets about their experience with euthanasia, you are likely to hear of animals who passed right before the euthanasia was to be performed. Many animals choose to go of their own initiative. As advanced yogis, they are able to slip out of their bodies when it is time.

Chapter 14

Animals Healing from Trauma

Animals who have been traumatized exhibit the same signs that people who have been traumatized exhibit. These signs of fear can be presented emotionally and physically. Hiding, numbing, growling, not eating, attacking, ignoring, over sleeping, and many other protective devices may come about after one is harmed. The spiritual notion that one is never harmed applies to the core of the soul. The body and mind and aspects of the soul can be hurt and do need to mend with patience and love. Love, care, honor, and respect are the essential ingredients when someone has been harmed. When an animal is taken care of properly and given love, care, honor, and respect, the wound can heal in layers. Trust in humans and other animals may be regained.

Listening to an animal and letting him or her know she/he has all the time and space in the world to feel whatever comes up is very important. Your animal may need an unconditionally loving witness as she/he shares her/his past challenges. Animals are masters at bringing out unconditional love in humans who are openhearted. Some animals prefer not to talk about the past and simply desire present love. Each animal will be different so ask and experiment. Keep an open, non-demanding dialogue active.

Healing can occur in many phases. An animal may seem to be at ease and then exhibit some original trauma symptoms. This is normal and natural. Simply continue to love, care, honor, and respect. Ask your animal friend about what she or he needs. Don't push for answers. Be gentle.

Animals who have been abandoned and abused will go through PTSD (Post-Traumatic Stress Disorder) just like humans. They need loyalty and consistent, positive treatment.

Chapter 15

Animals Speaking Out Loud

Many animals will practice saying words that they have heard. Many birds can speak in phrases and even in sentences. Dogs and cats have been known to use human language.

Brad Steiger and Sherry Hansen Steiger's book, *Cat Miracles* (2003) tells of cats who use words. This book relays the story of a cat, Yama, who could say, "Hell-Row Yama," (hello Yama) and "Wan nummies Mama, now!" The Steigers met this cat in person to verify this speaking claim before putting the information into print. Sure enough, they heard Yama talk to them in person with their own ears. My own cat, Jessie Justin Joy, has spoken a variety of words and phrases including "I love you". In a discussion with Penelope Smith, I learned that her beloved family member, Belinda the dog, also uses verbal language.

Chapter 16

Missing Animals Who Leave Home

The well-established animal communicator, Gina Palmer, once said, "Animals are never missing. Nobody is ever missing. Everyone is somewhere!" Gina went through a long adventure with her beloved friend Alex, a bird. Alex was Gina's best friend and they were inseparable. But Alex learned she could fly one day and took off.

This was not the first time a family member of Gina's had flown off. Her beloved family member, Spirit the dove, who was father of many, had created a little opening in his aviary. Spirit had flown miles away every day, always returning before Gina could discover this. One time, Gina went looking for Spirit in the aviary and he was gone. She asked one of his children about his whereabouts and learned of a little opening in the corner of the aviary. His child reported that Spirit took a daily trip for flying. This was surprising and news for Gina to hear. Gina then witnessed him flying off in the sky. Spirit knew how to navigate himself away and back.

Alex on the other hand did not. She had an adventure with some wild birds and learned that wild life is not like domestic life. She was not sure about how to feed herself. Via telepathic communication, Gina asked Alex to call out so someone would hear her. Gina put up posters of Alex. Alex called out. A woman heard her and called Gina who went to the woman's house. Alex flew from a high tree, landing at Gina's feet. The reunion was dear to both.

Animals leave home for a variety of reasons. Sonya Fitzpatrick, in her book *Cat Talk: The Secrets of Communicating with Your Cat* (2003), talks of a cat who is unhappy with the arrangements and finds a new home. Another cat is unhappy with the arrangements, receives a communication from her person that she will change the arrangements, and returns. If an animal is not fully honored she/he may choose to go somewhere else.

The animal tends to stay in touch with the person when this choice is made. Sometimes animals leave temporarily as a lesson is being called forth. Sometimes animals have temporary duties to serve another human, animal, or planetary elements, and nature. In this case an animal may leave and then come back.

Often, when an animal leaves, the communication waiting to come about from this happening is vital for the person. An animal does not leave randomly. There is always a cause. The cause may be spiritual, physical, mental, or emotional. It may be a combination of some or all of these elements. Asking the animal will often open up new possibilities of reunion.

Chapter 17

Rescued Animals

Rescued animals will exhibit the same signs that animals who are healing from trauma exhibit. You can work with them in the same way you work with animals who have endured any trauma.

The North Shore Animal League America in Port Washington, New York (www.nsalamerica.org) is a no-kill rescue and adoption center. Offering care, recovery, and help for animals who have been neglected, abused, or abandoned, the shelter provides medical care from minor to extreme. Approximately 25,000 animals are given love and aid each year. The animals are guided to loving homes and, if needed in the interim, temporary foster homes. Some of the rescued animals are taken in from other shelters that do not have the medical care and training that North Shore provides.

Because these animals are given help to heal their hearts as well as their bodies, those who come with the most horrific of abuse stories can turn around.

A lovely and peaceful being named Annabelle suffered from severe abuse. This sweet feline, drenched in gasoline and lit on fire, survived against horrific odds. In the beginning she would trust no human. After her medical needs were provided for and she was stable, one of the staff at NSALA fostered her. The foster-care person was very sensitive to her needs when she would hide after having a bad memory. Because of his patience, and in a short three-week time frame with home physical care, patience, great love, respect, and compassion, she began to trust humans again.

Hurt animals will receive love with human patience. Love and gratitude are the primary bases of telepathic communication. Many people who think they are not telepathic actually are. Many people pick up and respond to animals' thoughts and feelings even if they are not doing so with complete knowledge that they are. If you fully love an animal, you have the ability to help an animal in need with emotionally healing. If you fully love an animal, you have the ability to communicate with that animal.

Chapter 18

Animals Receiving Healing

Animals, like people, will have preferences. It is important to ask an animal if she/he prefers homeopathy, acupuncture, Western medicine, Eastern medicine, chiropractic, herbs, or Bach flowers based on availability in your geographical area. You can also ask an animal to tell you the outcome and effect of particular treatments offered. An animal is often able to understand the cause and effect of a particular vibration to his/her body. If you ask an animal about a pill, an operation, a food, or a supplement, the animal is likely to give you the physical, mental, emotional, and spiritual outcome to occur should he or she receive the specific treatment discussed. Some animals will be crystal clear on this topic. Others may not as their interest may not be on this subject matter. They may ask you to use your judgment in collaboration with medical professionals.

It is important to ask the animal if she/he is in favor of a particular practitioner. The vibration of the practitioner will affect the animal's experience of healing or not healing.

You may also discuss the value and purpose of the healing opportunity that is being presented to your animal friend and your family when an injury or illness occurs. Be sensitive of course. If the animal is using all of his or her energy for the recovery process, or if an animal has received anesthesia, it may not be the best time to talk. Remember to ask your animal if it is a good time to have a discussion.

Chapter 19

Animals Giving Healing

Many animals are healers. If an animal jumps on a person who is receiving a body work or energetic healing session, or places his/herself under a massage table, she/he is healing. You can trust your animals who are working as healers for people or other animals and thank them for their good work.

Chapter 20

Behavioral and Emotional Challenges

A. Assume Altruism is at Play

Animals are profoundly dedicated to their devotion toward you and will do whatever it takes to get your attention! Most often, what a person perceives to be a behavior problem is an act to call forth new awareness. For example, a cat might say to her person, "You must slow down and enjoy life or you will miss out and make yourself sick." First, the cat says this nicely. The person doesn't hear the telepathic suggestion.

Next, the cat takes to jumping on the person's work papers and desk, and purring and cuddling. The person thinks that his/her cat needs a lot of attention and misses the communication once again.

Finally the cat makes a crying sound. The person wonders why his/her cat is sad but keeps working.

As a last resort of completely selfless dedication the cat leaves a little piece of poop by her person's desk. She will do whatever it takes to get you to take care of yourself. Then the person says the cat has behavior problems. The cat keeps trying in love. These types of misunderstandings between person and animal companion are common.

If an animal is doing something to get your attention, assume that altruism is at play. You are likely overlooking an emotion or a need for either yourself or this animal (usually both) that requires your attention. An opportunity for harmony to be restored is being called forth via this learning opportunity. You can trust your animals are communicating the very best way they know how. I know a man who always thanks his cat for bringing him a mouse. As this man says, "He uses all his resources. He cannot go to the shopping mall when it is my birthday. I am grateful for his care and work in gifting me."

B. Maintain a Positive Perspective of Inquiry

Behind every behavior that is disruptive to someone else is a well-intended action or emotion. If you are going to discuss behaviors with animals, follow the same principle of empathetic witnessing and experiencing. Your job is to get into their world and understand their intentions in accordance with their soul purpose, needs, and good will. Once you do this, the possibility of a new way of doing things is much more specious. You know that when you try to argue, fix, or push a person into a way of being that is not his or her choice, you create friction.

This occurs with animals, too. It is more valuable to comprehend the animal's viewpoint, share your needs, and then create a mutual solution. Animals are willing to do this.

In some situations, problems are the result of different programming in the animal's genetic codes than in the human's codes. In these cases, working with a behaviorist is a wonderful way to create interspecies harmony. This could be relevant in house training a dog to be domestic, or learning to ride a horse, or helping a cat with litter problems. Behaviorism is a different topic than telepathic animal communication and can be studied in-depth with each animal species.

People have all kinds of communication mix-ups with animals. People also misinterpret challenges among animals within the same family when emotional problems are evident. Often, you can address these problems by speaking to the animals and discovering what it is they are wishing to accomplish! When an animal is upset, ask him or her if the problem is mental, physical, emotional, or spiritual.

Ask about each of these categories one at a time, giving the animal plenty of time to answer. Ask, for example, "Harry, are you chewing Jason's bone for emotional reasons?"

Harry might say, "I enjoy being the head dog and like to remind Jason that I am I the head dog."

You might thank Harry for letting you know, and then ask, "Harry, are you chewing Jason's bone for physical reasons?"

Harry might answer, "My mouth just loves to chew anything I can find but my purpose in specifically chewing Jason's bone is to make sure he knows I am head dog."

You can again thank Harry, and then ask, "Harry, are you chewing Jason's bone for spiritual reasons?"

Harry might say, "Yes, Jason is supposed to learn how to have self-confidence when he is not head dog. That is one of his tasks this lifetime. Later in his life he will become head dog when I am older and he will need patience plus confidence. I am helping to train him."

Thank Harry and ask, "Harry, are you chewing Jason's bone for mental reasons?"

Harry may say, "Yes, I have a challenge with needing to feel important and I will be working on overcoming this issue this lifetime. I had forgotten and thanks for reminding me."

Until you get a full picture of Harry's world it would be easy to blame Harry and/or make him wrong. Once you have a full understanding, you can see the rightness, too. You may look for a solution or you may find that what you thought was a problem is not. The animals may have this under management in their own domain!

C. Create Solution-Oriented Topics

Once you identify the positive intention behind an animal's actions you can discuss a solution that will serve everyone. Rest assured that when an animal is aiming to get a helpful message across, and the person at last comprehends, change is likely.

If you ask an animal or person, "How can we fulfill both our needs?" you elicit cooperation.

If you ask, "Will you stop it?" you are operating with intolerance and an arrogance that is unlikely to bring any positive results. You are assuming that your world is better and someone else should do what you think fit. In the world of harmonious relating, there are two sides to every story. It is in the inquiry into each side that a new solution shall be created, worthy of a deeper fulfillment for both involved.

D. Body Needs and Genetic Wiring

The body and the soul are not the same. While many humans forget this in the early years of an incarnation, some do not. Animals do not. Animals are very aware of the difference between a body, a mind, and a soul. A dog once turned his head to face his back legs and said "Hurry up!"

A soul can take on a body that is hard-code wired into particular physical and emotional tendencies. For example, a soul might wish to be cooperative but may be born into a body that is highly jumpy, prone to running, and anxious. For this reason, the dog will need patience, love, and assistance in training his or her body to cooperate.

Don't read motives into others' experiences. There are many reasons for why a soul takes on a particular body which are related to gifts of learning and awakening. A soul usually takes on the gift of a body for the benefit of those around her/him in addition to the benefits to her/himself. A cooperative soul could take on an anxious body to practice patience or to teach others the practice of patience.

Assume the best at all times, ask questions, and work from a valuing of harmony rather than a valuing of wrong/right or good/bad. In this, animal communication can flow. Because animals speak from love and unconditional realms, making a behavior wrong will not touch or reach the place from where animal's perspective exists. Such an outlook will block the door to communicating. Stepping consistently into an animal's world view will open the door. The more you do so, the greater your capacity to recognize that animals have done this with you and for you all along! Many of you will come to see that your souls are the same while your perspectives are differently informed.

Remember that an animal will see the body and personality traits as something to work with rather than to judge. People can learn unconditional self-love from coming to understand this animal point of view.

E. Emotional Learning

When an animal and/or a person has a soul contract or simply a need to learn a particular emotional lesson, a behavior challenge will serve as the catalyst for this to occur.

A behavior problem may be a messenger. The message is often one that will take the person into a deeper realm of peace, joy, love, faith, trust, grace, abundance, kindness, compassion, patience, or another life quality. In assisting a person to delve deeper into a life quality the animal also deepens his or her relationship with this quality.

An example is a cat who jumps on someone's toes early in the morning. A person might think the cat gets up way too early and needs to learn to sleep. Upon greater introspection, a person might realize that s/he is waking up early him/herself and spinning his/her thoughts into useless anxiety. The cat is playfully pouncing to bring the person out of the anxious mind and back into playfulness.

Often, when a person faces that which is emotionally disharmonious in his or her self, an animal's behavior shifts.

F. Spiritual Passages for All Involved

A behavior problem may show up in an animal in your life to assist you with learning care, nurturance, patience, compromise, respect, kindness, and a multitude of other qualities. The invitation that animals offer you to return to the unconditional realms is astounding and full.

A horse got ill and no longer wanted to race even though he was a winner. He told his person that he was unhappy and so was she. They were both controlling themselves and their lives to look good rather than unfolding into true happiness. The horse explained that the only way to recovery was for both of them to let go and rediscover the value and meaning of life. A new path and new view were the way to healing.

This was not what the woman wanted to hear because her identity was wrapped up in her horse's success. However, she loved her horse and this caused her to contemplate the gift that he was giving her.

G. Mental Frameworks in Transition

A behavior problem may show up to invite you to shift a rigid mental belief that no longer serves you. A woman called because it was important to her that both of her cats get along. To her, this would be a symbol of peace. When I spoke to the cats they explained that both of them as well as the woman were involved in personal leanings. As souls they all loved one another and on the personality level they were working through necessary challenges for everyone's growth. The woman was to learn patience in all situations. She was to release thoughts of fixing others and focus on her own layers of self instead. She was to replace the notion that something was wrong with the concept that everything is right on track. This was a lesson that had shown up in this woman's life many times. The scenario with the cats was there to help her learn in a gentle, loving way.

Chapter 21

Wild Animals

Telepathic communication with wild animals is done in the same way as with domestic animals. Of course, a variety of wild animals should not be approached in the physical. Although Ramana Maharshi was able to converse safely with snakes, most of us are not at this level of ability. Speaking with animals does not shift particular species' natural needs to protect themselves or to eat as carnivores. Nor does it necessarily alleviate fears some animals have learned to have of humans.

In addition, animals have physical languages that one needs to learn to be in their world with any safety. For example, bears and lions can misread your body language if you do not understand theirs'. Be practical and wise. Unless you are trained to communicate with animals via physical expertise in their body language (for example, you are trained as a lion trainer) it is best to keep telepathic communication as your main operant with wild life who could be dangerous to you in the physical realm. Several people known to have lived with lions or bears who their bodies in the end. While there was likely a soul contract for life to transform, be careful with yourself. One bear lover knew his time was coming when one of his friends was starving. He chose to stay among the bears anyway and did get eaten. However, Charlie Vandergaw continues to live in the Alaskan wilderness among bears and has remained safe so far. (The Man Who Lives With Bears www.youtube.com/watch?v=TSOKW6V6Bi8.)

Remember that the body-mind-personality is programmed from years of survival mechanisms. You can understand this from your own life. Your soul intention and your body-mind-personality cannot always cooperate without first deconditioning, and second, relearning. If you have done personal growth work, you have noticed emotional, physical, and mental habits that you inherited that no longer serve you. In the same way, the predator-prey and survival mechanisms in a wild animal's body are very strong. An animal may love a person but also respond instinctually with body habits. Lion trainers agree that a miscommunication with the body can give a lion an idea that you are attacking a lion. This can be fatal. The lion will respond accordingly and immediately to body language even though no emotional animosity is present. Animals do not view life and death the way that many people do. As mentioned earlier, animals experience their bodies as body-mind-personalities and as temporary costumes.

I have spoken to dogs and cats who have had trouble controlling their bodies due to innate wiring. I have talked to dogs who are very wound up and jump on people when they mean no harm.

When you reach out from the telepathic heart to wild animals, who you ascertain to be safe in the physical realms, they will know. Often they will come to greet you if it is your desire. Dolphins, whales, turtles, hawks, ravens, and all kinds of birds, squirrels, and many other species have been known to approach and befriend loving humans.

Take into account that wild animals do not have the same orientation to life as domestic ones so they may communicate with more feelings and less words. Be prepared to view the world in new ways when you connect with animals who live in environments unfamiliar to you.

Chapter 22

Cross-Species Animal Friends

Thanks to the Internet, photography of animal friends from different species is accessible. When the tsunami hit Thailand near the beginning of the twenty-first century, animals of many species were safe. The animals could sense the tsunami coming and had gotten word out from one species to another. Consequently, many went to the highlands and survived. In another heartwarming story, a very young hippo was separated from his mother in Kenya after the 2004 tsunami and was found on the beach. He was brought to Haller Park where he befriended a 130-year-old male tortoise who took over mothering. See the following website for details: http://www.lafarge.co.ke/wps/portal/ke/4_A_3_9-WildlifeSanctuary.

The Collitos were unsure if the kitten, Cassie, was safe near the crow, but as days went on and they documented the kitten-crow interactions on video, the nature of the relationship was revealed. The crow was attending to the kitten, feeding him worms in the mouth, protecting him from going out in the street, and ensuring his livelihood. Over time, these two friends proved to be inseparable. Living together, playing together, and spending their days together, they were as close as close can be. When the Collitos began to take the cat inside at night, his crow friend, Moses, would wait for him each morning, making eye contact with Ann through the window. Ann experienced this as Moses letting her know that he trusted Ann and Wallace with his beloved friend. See the following website for more information: http://www.earthlings.org/kin/kinship.html

At a retirement farm for female elephants in Tennessee, every elephant finds a best friend. In the case of Tarra and Bella, the two best friends are elephant and dog. They walk, eat, play, and sleep together. (*Tarra & Bella: The Elephant and Dog Who Became Best Friends*, a children's book by Carol Buckley)

A hamster, who is given to a snake for lunch at a zoo, becomes friends with the snake. They kiss. They cuddle. They remain companions. www.youtube.com/watch?v=-IG4kceZBWA&feature=channel. The trust in one another is obvious.

A cat named Snaggle Puss takes over the mothering of a baby rabbit named Bubbles. She cleans, feeds, carries, and fully parents this little one who sadly lost his own mother at one week old. Bubbles nurses in a cuddle pile next to his kitten siblings. www.youtube.com/watch?v=04RZrf3-Mgo&feature=related. The kindness and the care is apparent.

A cat decides to adopt and nurse a baby red panda who had been abandoned. A zookeeper was keeping the panda in an incubator when the keeper's cat, on her own initiative, decided to take over. She had two kittens and brought the panda into her litter, seeing he was in need.

www.youtube.com/watch?v=31LH7ZBYgQc&NR=1

A monkey in India becomes the mother of an orphaned kitten.

www.youtube.com/watch?v=fhHVMKYzG_s&feature=related

The list of species comprising mixed-species animal families and human-animal families goes on and on. Somehow, there is no species language barrier when love is the focus. In the same fashion, animals who meet people or other animals of different cultural languages do not face the barriers that humans sometimes face with each other. When the language is one of the telepathic heart, the translation naturally occurs.

Do not assume that all this cross-species parenting is random. The monkey who is mothering the cat is alert to her role in helping humanity to uncover her/his own disguises and find the heart below the surface. Once again, animals are, on purpose, intelligent and alert in multiple ways all at once.

Addendum

Previews from Dr. Laurie Moore's

The Cat's Reincarnation: Transformative Encounters with Animals Animals communicate as heart touching heart. They listen as witnesses and discover how each one who greets them touches them. The offering that animals extend to us is the same invitation many an enlightened master has presented. In order to speak, feel, hear, see, know their language we are required to melt into the unconditional realm of our own hearts. This is the only way to be fully reached by an animal friend. This is because animals resonate to the beat of the earth, the tide of the ocean, the sun, the moon, and the natural energies that are birthing each moment.

What I have to share with you next are two personal shamanic roads I have traveled. These sharings come from my book *The Cat's Reincarnation: Transformative Encounters with Animals* (2013). These excursions were offered to me in the act of surrendering to the guidance available in the communications from some of my animal friends. My hope is that they will move you into an arena of soul that you are welcome to take to spark your own journey. Next, you may be the one to share your own story!

The Yellow-Winged Peace Moth

As a therapist I have made many appearances as a public speaker. One of my favorite topics to discuss has been "Eleven Steps to Guaranteed Success and Happiness." In 2004, as the Keynote Speaker for The Women in Business Expo put on by the *Santa Cruz Sentinel,* I prepared to give this favorite talk of mine. As I was getting ready to head to the podium, a beautiful yellow-winged moth landed on my books.

"Are you here to speak with me?" I asked.

"Yes, I have come to assist with your talk."

"What do you wish for me to know?"

"The information you impart at your talk is SECONDARY. It is good for the people to learn about series of steps to guaranteed happiness and success, but that is not your PRIMARY purpose. The reason you have been called to give this talk is to be in peace. As you stand in the vibration of unconditional peace, so too will the audience."

"Okay," I agreed with great gratitude. The moth and I arranged to be in each other's hearts throughout the talk. As I gave the talk I was in peace.

After the talk I was sure that my entire life had been used well, that I had made all the right decisions, that everything was in perfect order, place, and time, and that I was doing exactly what I agreed to do on Earth. This was a huge relief to me, as I have always been full of goals and ambitions. It turned out that my only purpose is to BE love and peace and joy, and doing this to the best of my ability is success. My moth Beloved had taught me.

After the speech I returned to my chair. My moth was gone. Several minutes later she flew over to me, seemingly out of nowhere, and landed on my arm! We looked at each other in great love, awe, and gratitude. The little eyes were so precious.

"Thank you, my Love," said my friend, yellow-winged moth, to me.

Two bugs appeared and off went the three.

I was taken to such peace that I knew I would always be in peace. My life was forever changed. I had been invited to live in the unconditional.

Red-tailed Hawk Day

Last night I fell asleep by the screen door. Ray and I don't sleep outside because it's too risky to have feline Jessie Justin Joy outside at night. The three of us like to be together. I felt the spirits beckon me outside, and I was as outside as I could be. My heart was there. There was a song in the air. I could hear the tones of C. Bass, tenor, alto, and sopranos were all cooperating.

The night became my lover, holding me. I could feel the entire night truly holding me, and I was in love. I could feel the night wrap me up like a soft lavender blanket and my skin felt nourished. I felt nourished to the core. I was mesmerized by the sweet scent held out to me as a gift from the wild ginger. I was pulled home like a child to a father's chest, by the love peering through the gleaming eyes of the sky, the stars. Ray was downstairs working but I could feel his soothing energy wrapped into the night, too. I remembered that all that matters to me is to follow this Divine Love. I delight in all the service projects, but it is following this Divine Love in nature that feeds me most completely.

The next morning the mountains promised that I am them. "You will be a strong warrior, as strong as we are if you feed yourself well. Take good care of your body. Eat good food. Eat our strength through your gaze." As I listened, I breathed the rich greens that covered the hills into myself. I felt myself remember that once I was an Indian Boy. I wondered if it was my soul that lived an Indian Boy's life. Perhaps the memory came from something else. Maybe there was an Indian Boy in my ancestral line, recorded in my DNA.

I was walking up and down the hill, feeling very tired from the output of energy over the last couple of weeks. Feline JJJ doesn't do as many laps as I do, so he decided to wait at the bottom of the hill after we shared three. A grapefruit hung low from the small tree, catching my eye. I went to pick it and said, "Thank you."

As I thanked the tree, my heart was filled with the warmth of a tree saying "thank you" in return. Sharing this gratitude, I felt complete. Lime green, evergreen, dark green, and pastel green surrounded me.

Next, the phone rang, and after I answered it I was in a different world. Someone called about an argument they had with their spouse. The person's voice scratched against me. I felt like the two of us were C# and D on the phone, silently competing. I wanted her to feel happier and she wanted me to feel her pain. I felt tired out. Back outside, doing laps up and down the hill, I was complaining to myself: "I need more energy. What happened? The hawks have been gone for almost a week."

Then he flew in front of me: the Red-tailed Hawk with beautiful wings and big feet. I watched him go straight in front and then up to the sky, circling to my right. His pink, grey, and red colors took my heart up into the sky with him. I was on the ground and I was flying at the same time. "Come here, if you would," I asked. "Would you teach me how to be stronger?"

At once he came, circling above me. Loud buzzing sounds began—it was the dragonflies: three of them coming to dance by me as I watched the hawk. The sun patted my forehead. I stretched my arms out as I looked up, and he was now straight above me, still for a moment, with his wings also stretched.

"Thank you, thank you. What does life ask of me?" I queried.

"We ask that you be very quiet and content and listen to us. We are stronger than you can imagine and we have a message for you now. Come back to us."

"Please teach me to be a real medicine woman," I said.

"A medicine woman uses Holy Scriptures and objects to woo others back into their own flight...back to themselves beyond you...back to who they are."

"Yes, and am I doing a good job?"

"There's more. Go deeper. When we are missing from you, you must go deeper to call us back in gently. When you don't see us, go further into your own magic. Then watch how quickly we return." The red-tail was gone, but a vision of him above a lake came blaring kindly and alarmingly into my mind. He looked like he was swooping down lower.

"You still give too much of yourself away," he cautioned me. I could hear him though his body was not near. I rubbed my palm with my other hand, feeling the different muscles all doing their jobs in one hand.

"How do I know what limits and boundaries to set?"

"Be more careful. Spend more time with us and you will learn. It's your turn."

"What can I offer you in return?"

"You can only offer yourself. There is nothing more and nothing less."

"What do I do next?"

"You must sit by a creek and let us come through the back door. It is our time to come to you."

I began to make plans to drive out to Felton and visit Fall Creek. I stopped in my own tracks, recalling something I had read in a book by Raymon Grace titled *The Future is Yours: Do Something About It!* (2003). He said you can connect to the water anywhere, from wherever you are. Instead of getting in the car, going to the gas station, and driving a ways, I sent my soul to the creek.

There I heard chimes and high-pitched sounds. A cool breeze smiled both at me and in me, causing my heart to relax. I lay on the ground, feeling massaged by the sun collected in the earth. I began to rejuvenate.

"You have lost your soul memory. You are only halfway there. You must listen deeper. Listen to the night. Listen to the forest. Listen to the day. Listen to us and not to anyone else. We will help you. We are clear and we are in everything. Hear us."

I began to cry. "I am here, Mother of Life. Here I am and I will run to you as JJJ runs to me. I will listen."

"Have you noticed that every song and dance, everything you did for us has always stayed with you and come back to you? There is no past that isn't here."

"Yes."

"Then soak your face in the creek. Be cared for. Be served."

I did and it was so cool that my energy began to come back. I saw an image of an owl when I put my head under.

Bathed and nourished, held and supported, suddenly rejuvenated, I lay in the water. I have spent many occasions in water with my 3D body: the creeks, the oceans, the rivers, and the lakes...and now, right from my house without going anywhere, I was fully relieved and cleansed and rejuvenated. The water had come to me.

"Thank you to the water all over the planet," I said. "You are the life within us all. I love you forever. You are my hero. Thank you. May you be loved by everyone forever. I send you my love and I find myself home in you."

I could feel Red-tailed Hawk and Owl alive in my being. Flaming strength had been lit in my heart. My feet were alive and wise as they felt the clay-baked earth and heard the message Red-tailed Hawk sent to Earth and me. I sat down in a soft outdoor chair, astounded that I could go from burnt out and lifeless to fully strong in an hour. It was letting them guide me. It was letting the hawk and the guides take me that gave me strength. There is no more strength in anything I do alone. It must come from the guidance of the wise ones.

JJJ sat under my chair. We breathed. We were content and in awe and in love with the laughter streaming through the air. A neighbor revved up a very loud motorcycle and went past us in a blurry grey uproar, down the hill, around, and back up.

We stayed close to the ground and stayed peaceful. I sent love to the neighbor. He was expressing himself in the way that was working for him. All was fine. There was room for us both in our different modes. I heard the canyon echo back to him.

"RRrr," went the motorcycle.

"RRrr," said the canyon.

"WOORP!" shouted the motorcycle.

"WOORP!" shouted the canyon. My heart was amazed at how powerful our messages are. What we sing, sings back. JJJ and I were being held in the life mirror.

I saw the neighbor approaching our shared driveway. His friend's truck arrived also so I decided to camouflage myself the way JJJ does. I could not talk and maintain this strength of silence.

I lay on my back on the ground between the shrubs and vines. JJJ was with me. I made myself flat and still.

"Thanks for coming all the way up here," I heard one say.

"It's a miracle I didn't barf," his friend said in response. Why did I have neighbors whose miracles were stuff like this?

I remembered what Gina told me. "Anyone who shows up in your reality is there because you called them there." I chuckled silently.

I was growing stronger. Something was brewing inside me, and it felt stronger than anything I had ever known myself to be before. I was feeling the hawk and the owl in my muscles and blood in a most present, awe-inspiring, and enlivening way. I realized that the neighbor and his friend had hawk and owl in them also. We shared this energy. When they passed, it lessened, so I knew that being together made it more powerful. It was not mine alone. I felt more respect. There was something to learn in the judgments that had arisen between us silently over time. There was something better beckoning us, and Red-tailed Hawk was calling this forth.

JJJ and I remained in the silence, and all of a sudden Red-tailed Hawk flew right over me. JJJ was under a chair. I was out in the open to the sky though camouflaged on the sides of my body. Red-tailed Hawk was only a few feet above with a red beak.

JJJ ran and I was taken over by complete feminine love. This hawk must have been a female. I sat up quickly to protect JJJ but noticed he had run from under the chair to the open and was hunting. Was JJJ safe?

I felt my fear thoughts disrupt the smooth, complete, vast, and safe love.

"Will you keep JJJ safe?" I asked both Red-tailed Hawk and life itself.

"There are only thoughts of love and thoughts of fear. Your thoughts choose realities," was the answer that came back.

The day was getting ready to come to a close and turn into the night. With great grace and smoothness one becomes the other. JJJ sat safely on the deck with the loving sun filtering from his yellow eyes into the world. I went to put a load of towels in the washing machine.

"Go down to the deck behind the house," my guides instructed.

"Maybe JJJ and I should go for round three of lessons with Red-tailed Hawk," I said.

"There is no reason to do that. Always follow your instincts. Your instincts tell you to go to the back deck, so there you shall go."

I went to the back deck and lay in a chair. I felt that love was coming from me and love was coming to me. All the love that ever was in the universe was having a reunion with her/himself in me. I was no one but everyone, and this could be happening in all who allowed it now.

"Our work today is complete," Red-tailed Hawk said. "Listen to the message of now." She was gone.

I was enveloped in perfect love. All was complete. The day was right on track and knew exactly what was supposed to have happened. Everything was in its right time and place. I felt perfect love. My job was done just as it needed to be done. What I yearned for was here now.

———

Two days ago a new client, Jake, came in. He told me that a woman had been caustic to him and had screamed and hit him when he had been loving and kind. He confused himself by still feeling attached to her. I felt he was telling the truth. I felt he had been very kind.

He told me of his land called "Two Grandmothers" because two grandmother spirits lived there and walked by him, one on each side, at night, with great love. He told me of the hummingbirds who flew around his face with great love and his friends the ravens. His visit to my office was a blessing and informed me that the world was changing.

I told him that it is harder to let go of someone who is mean to us than someone who is just not a good fit. This is because the soul yearns for resolution that is kind. When there is none, the personality feels a desire to go back and solve it.

"So close your eyes," I said to the kind man, "and imagine a woman that you will meet in the future. You can feel her now. This woman will love you with great love and kindness like the love and kindness you give. She will love you like the hummingbirds and the grandmothers. From now on, when your mind focuses on the woman who hurt you, immediately shift your mind to the woman who will love you. You will find her this way, first inside yourself and then outside."

I knew he could make this work. It is how I found Ray, and this man had great love in his heart to make it work.

Suddenly, while lying on the chair on the deck in perfect love, I felt this man and his two grandmothers sending me so much love that I began to cry. All the years of feeling that my work was not worthy enough faded. I was helping people in real ways. All my complaining, that the clients took and did not give enough back, was untrue. Many beautiful souls held me in gratitude in their hearts. Everything is and will always be perfect.

I was about to get up and go inside when I heard a noise. A sparrow landed right in my gaze. "Hello sweet bird," I said. He looked at me and preened himself for a while. I realized that my job was not complete.

"Guides of mine and guides of all my clients I ever met, I send this message now. You are held in the arms of The Divine Mother and you are forever loved. All is well in your worlds," I said aloud.

Then I heard the great wail. I heard the deep-seated big sob from the pit of the stomach that lives in the world. I held this sob in my arms like a baby, covered her/him in a blanket, rocked him/her back and forth and said, "You are loved now forevermore. Hear this today."

"Dial them up. Wake them up. Please, get their attention any way you can," I said to the birds and spirits. "Help them."

"We are doing all we can. Now it is your humanity that must listen."

Then I remembered what Marsha, the radio interviewer, told me on the air. She said that a hawk came to visit her and took a bath in her bird bath just a foot away from her and they were immediate friends. I felt appreciation for Marsha. I thought gratefully of Gina teaching her class to people so they can hear animals more clearly. I realized that so many of us are in love with animals and life now that everyone can catch on.

So I listen deep into the love that the birds have woven into the sky and continue.

Conclusion

Animal communication begins with the love-born desire to befriend animal family members and friends at a deeper level. We wish to see through their eyes, feel through their hearts, sense through their sensations, and hear through their ears. Once we embark on this journey we find that another inherent gift is exposed. We are taken into the depth of our unconditional nature, the joy of our universal heart, the oneness that holds all our experiences. We are home in a profound way of peace.

This experience can only be found in the journey of trial and error, stepping into the process, and having a unique individual series of encounters between self and animals. Animal communication is available by jumping into the unknown using the exercises and guidelines offered. As you give yourself the gift of this life-trail, available to you forever, you will find your own wisdom and fulfillments. The animals will bring gems and treasures to your soul.

Message from Feline Jessie Justin Joy

I have assisted my Mother, Laurie, with writing parts of this course and would like to address those who are studying.

In this lifetime, I am again Laurie's cat son and she is my human Mother. This arrangement gives us access to great joy, fun, and even some playful fame. However, this is a fraction of our relationship. I am actually a teacher of unconditional kindness and love as well as a personal guide who has walked the planet many times for millions of years. I am a good friend to Mother Earth. Laurie and I have re-found each other again and again so that I can guide her and help her to make teachings fresh and new each time we meet. She greets me as a loving friend each time. Our familiarity with one another is big. I have insisted that she practice and view life situations freshly, again and again, so that her teaching of love never goes stale. I hold a curtain and ask her to open it.

Together we laugh and play, undo karma, speak of dreams, and learn mystery. I carefully guide her and attend to her in all she does, finding a way to coax her out of any lethargy and helping her to see as I do. I see the one Lord of one and all in all beings and circumstances that pass through and as life. We work as one now.

I wish to address humanity at this time. Animals come to help you in goodness and as your guides. We do not come to be selfish or slow household matters down. We listen in on everything and push you to reach your potential. Our mission is our choice. We live it out with endearment toward you whom we gather in our hearts and arms.

I am a mystic of my own choosing. Make no mistakes. I am here as watchful guide to tend and listen to many by watching how they think. I urge them to get on with their new ways and let the karma off the clock because the clock does tick. We animals are never here to burden you or one another but here to teach, cuddle, play, be in joy, and gather fascination in life. We are tender souls.

Please stop trying to guide us; speak to us in reverence to find out who we are and how we have come with guidance to help you. We are powerful and wonderful teachers full of intelligence and pride, here to walk the earth by your side. Do not color our picture with your own needs or anger. Give us gentleness and do not hurry. Sink into our teachings, which are of the real world that has lasted and will last much longer than your current pictures of life. Humanity is a species. Like other species it may have a beginning and an end. I do not say this to disappoint you but rather to reach you with wisdom. Come join the human family in a humble way, a forgiving way, and a learning way.

Humanity has lost course a bit, involved in all kinds of games, twists, spins, and expectations of one another that really don't matter. This causes you all to bump heads. Instead, be quiet a little and see we are here to coax you, nudge you, and urge you back to a fuller humanity. The course of the Earth has many years to come and humanity may continue to play a part. However, you have gotten estranged and lost from the Mother herself. Take time to talk to the moon, the sun, and have fun for a while to remember who you are. I am Jessie Justin Joy, your friend, beloved, and loving one. I love.

Introductory Techniques and Exercises

1. **Be in a State of Gratitude**

   Animals communicate through the universal language of the heart. If the intellect is not founded in a heartfelt vibration you will not connect well with your animal. If you speak from your universal heart your animal will feel this. The quickest route to the universal heart is gratitude. Sit silently and focus on everything you can think of for which you are grateful. Notice what you feel when you focus on gratitude. Once you are in a sate of gratitude send some of that gratitude to an animal friend by focusing on him or her in your heart. Notice how this makes you feel. While this step may seem simple it is the most important step in animal communication. It is the foundation upon which all other steps will take place.

Journaling Topics

Seven experiences with animals for which I am grateful and why

Seven animals for whom I am grateful and why

---

2. Perceive Through Your Heart

To truly receive what your animal wishes to tell, you must listen through your heart instead of only your mind. Let your mind work with your heart. Sit quietly and ask to receive communication from your animal friend with your heart. Be aware of the information that comes when you focus receptively on your animal with your heart. This information may come in pictures. It may come in words. It may come in feelings. It may come in an awareness of vibration intentions. It may come in colors, tones, and shades. Without analyzing, making wrong, or making right, simply be aware of what you perceive.

Journaling Topics

Next time I wish to be in my heart I will use a set of tools that work best for me. Here is my list:

A song or piece of music that takes me into my loving heart is …

A picture that takes me into my loving heart is …

A thought that takes me into my loving heart is …

A place that takes me into my loving heart is …

A plant that takes me into my loving heart is …

An activity that takes me into my loving heart is …

> A memory that takes me into my loving heart is …
>
> An individual animal that takes me into my loving heart is …
>
> An animal species that takes me into my loving heart is …
>
> A movie that takes me into my loving heart is …
>
> An act of service that takes me into my loving heart is …

3. Ask Questions

Asking questions opens the door for another to share himself or herself. In the same way that you ask questions to get to know a person, ask questions to get to know your animal.

Examples include: "How are you? How can I make your life as happy as possible? Is there anything you would like me to know? What is your favorite activity?"

> **Journaling Topics**
>
> Questions I would like to ask my animal friend

4. Ask Questions in the Positive

Animals' language is based upon what is. "Isn't, doesn't, why not" are not part of their worlds. Animals are aware of what is. Convert any questions that enter your mind in the negative to the positive. For example, instead of "Why don't you come inside when I call you?" ask "What are you experiencing when you stay outside after I call you?"

Remember, your animal friend is living in the experience of his or her reality just as you are living in yours. You are always doing something and that is where your focus goes. Your animal friend is always doing something, being somewhere, feeling something, and that is where her/his experience exists. She or he is not "not doing" something. That way of thinking is based on the notion that your animal friend should fit your design. This kind of thinking will not build harmony or trust in relationships with people or animals. Making yourself available to understand another's point of view and experience will build harmony and trust.

Journaling Topics

List of questions arising in my mind in the negative to be converted to the positive

Conversions Formula:

> What you want is the opposite of what you don't want?
>
> Write down what you do want.
>
> Ask a question about your animal's experience of what she or he desires.
>
> Let your animal know what you want.
>
> Find a way to incorporate your animal's joys and your needs into a compromise or a new plan that brings joy to both of you.

5. Ask Your Animal Friend About His or Her Life Purpose

Although many people forget their past lives and their self-selected life purpose for a current incarnation, animals usually remember. Ask your animal friend about what his or her life purpose is. She or he will answer in one word or one phrase. Knowing his or her purpose will help you to fully respect the being you are living with. Examples of purposes of animals I have known are "to be happy," "to assist my friend with her life," "to help people laugh," "to play," "to supervise my family's affairs," "to make life feel good for those around me," "to protect my family," "to dream in new realities," "to bring in angelic realms," "to experience life as a canine after being a person many times," "to love."

> **Journaling Topics**
>
> Answers that came in feelings, thoughts, sounds, lights when I inquired about my animal friend's purpose

6. Ask for Clues about Accuracy

The answers that come to you about an animal may come from the animal or from your expectations. As a therapist I have learned to check for accuracy regarding my assumptions. I might perceive a person's experience inaccurately based on how I, myself, would experience life with their circumstances. To avoid this type of projection I ask my clients for their own descriptions of their experiences. By practicing readings with friend's animals and asking the friends about the information you receive you will get clues about the accuracy of your perceptions.

> **Journaling Topics**
>
> Signs of my Accuracy (check below if you are willing):
>
> ___ I am willing to focus on the ways that I am accurate and use any ways I am not accurate as learning tools.

> ___ I am willing to take five minutes of silence right now to send gratitude to myself for doing my best.
>
> ___ I am willing to send gratitude to life for giving me these experiences of animal communication.
>
> ___ I am willing to keep practicing and improve as I do.

7. Test for Accuracy Inwardly as Well as Outwardly

Many people get clues about the truth of a situation. We must use inner tests as well as outer tests for accuracy. Everyone's body and mind has ways of letting the soul in on the level of accuracy presented in a situation. Some people get goose pimples upon hearing something that rings real. Some people get a calm feeling in the heart. The opposite is also true. When something is not true some people get a queasy feeling in the stomach or a repeating thought that they are not accurate. Pay attention to your own signs. As you do your next animal reading, make notes on signs that pointed toward accuracy and signs that pointed away from accuracy.

> **Journaling Topics**
>
> Inner signs of accuracy
>
> Inner signs of inaccuracy
>
> Thank you to all signs for being teachers.

8. Experience Speaking to a Species as a Whole

While each animal has a unique personality, each species shares some common talents, focuses, ways of perceiving life, and values. For example, dolphins exist in a vibration of unconditional joy. Felines value their lives in other dimensions equally to their experiences here and are experts at dreaming realities into existence. Canines value loyalty and altruism and feel happily obliged to protect. Whales hold the energy of oneness. Elephants are group masters at creating tribes and families in harmonious ways. Hummingbirds live in Divine joy. Lizards know Mother Earth to be a friend. To learn more about animal species who are attractive to you, focus on your heart, ask the sun and the moon to guide you to the animals, and ask them to energetically share their worlds with you. Some of you will be able to do this when you are miles apart from the animals on the 3D. Others will find that physical proximity is important.

> **Journaling Topics**
>
> Which Species will I speak to?
>
> What did they tell me about themselves?
>
> How did their vibration feel to me?
>
> Did they send me images of their daily lives?
>
> Did I receive feelings about some of their intentions and values for being alive?
>
> What can I emulate from this species?
>
> Remember to thank them for speaking with you.

9. Ask for Confirmation in the 3D World

Not sure if I had a highly imaginative world of my own or an ability to receive messages from whales, I asked the whales to bring me a confirmation sign. Ask and you shall receive! Upon my arrival in Molokai, I had no idea that whales were in the vicinity. Within a minute of asking whales to bring a sign, one jumped parallel out of the water, flopped back, and proceeded to wave her tail for a very long time! It felt like thirty minutes but I was so taken by the experience that I am not sure of the exact duration. Another time, when doubt had a hold of me, I walked on a trail and sent a message of love to a lizard. The lizard raced up my body of his own initiative. He stayed on my back for a good portion of my hike. Send out a prayer to life for confirmation and be open to whatever form it arrives in.

Journaling Topics

My own confirmation stories—to be filled out at any time

(Be patient and trust they will come in the perfect ways and times for you. That may be in an hour or it may be in four years. There is no right or wrong.)

---

10. Practice Being

Learn how to simply "be" and you will naturally bond more deeply with the animals. Sit in silence. Focus on your heart. Your eyes can be opened or closed. Listen to the beat of your heart. Feel your heart. Keep your breaths going in and out deeply. Fill up your entire abdomen and chest and then fully release the air out.

Journaling Topics

> My experience of "being"

11. Share Your Animal-Friend's World

Spend a day with your friend. Aim to listen through his ears, travel through her eyes, and feel through the vibrations of his or her body. Know that everyone on this planet has a job to do. Something that may appear to be foolish or disruptive to your personal plans may be very much on purpose for an animal.

Humans have a made a mess of the natural permaculture design that animals practice. When an animal is picking at her fur she is trying to get a toxin out of her body. When a gnat was swarming around fruit in our home, I noticed the fruit she chose was rotting and needed to be put in the compost. When I put the rotting fruit in the compost, the gnats were happy to leave the fresh fruit for us. When an animal is crying for apparently no reason, be honest. Most likely, a human in your house is in emotional distress which your animal friend is vocalizing. The animals are often very altruistic and they are devoted in their tasks. Like youth, they also tend to mirror the vibrations of the adults in a house.

When I have listened to Jessie instead of my own mental frameworks of how things should be, he has spared me of future disease and taken me back to the Divine lap of health, love, and peace again and again, Many times he has insisted I leave the office and go get fresh air. Out of his insistence all my books are being written. If I had not listened to his side of the story, I would have thought he was just being annoying when he jumped on my desk and got in my way, meowing loudly. I would have missed the beautiful gift of his tenacious service.

Journaling Topics

Is there a behavior an animal has demonstrated towards which I have been intolerant? Am I willing to trade in my intolerance for curiosity and inquiry?

When I ask my animal about her or his experience and intention of this particular behavior, what pictures, feelings, words, or intentional vibrations do I find? When I consult other sources on animals (holistic vets, animal communicators, friends with the same species of animal living with them) what do I learn?

When I look in my own heart, do I find something my animal is trying to help me with, by engaging in a particular behavior?

What is my new plan for working with this behavior?

Exercise

Spend some time with no agenda and no questions, simply being in the presence of your beloved animal. If she or he chooses to go outside, go with him/her. If he or she chooses to play, play also.

Letting my animals desire's lead the way, I felt

_____

When I simply take time to be with my animal, I feel

_____

12. Ask for Assistance

We are all here to help each other. Pay attention to yourself. There are times when you will need outside assistance.

Journaling Topics

Whose help do I need: a vet, a friend, my angels, an animal communicator, a dog trainer, a book?

Who I need to speak to _____

Day I will call them _____

13. Allow Messages to be Poetic Metaphors in Motion

Not everything is liner and literal. Begin to hear the metaphor of all existence speaking through the animals.

Exercise

Sit quietly in a place where you can be alone. Close your eyes and allow yourself to feel, hear, sense, see, and smell all the sounds, words, pictures and images, vibrations, and scents. Be aware as they come and go. Let them come and go and inspire you. Let them come and go without doing anything with them. Let them come and go and touch you. Let them come and let them go.

14. Receive Medical Assistance from Trained Providers

If you have a medical question regarding your animal, consult with someone who has studied the bodies of that species. Vets offer a wide range of skills. There are homoeopathists, naturopaths, herbalists, acupuncturists, and regular Western veterinarians who can assist your animal. The body is an intricate tool and deserves top notch treatment.

Journaling Topics

Signs that my animal may need some physical assistance form a professional

---

15. Love and Respect Yourself with All Your Strengths & Your Areas that Need Improvement

Animals have an amazing ability to keep focusing on what is good about them and you. Whenever an animal has told me about strength or a weakness s/he embodies s/he has told me with great respect for all that is. The animals accept themselves with respect in place of judgment. As you learn to communicate, use there non-judgmental reverence for whatever is as inspiration. To truly understand another you must see through his eyes and walk in her shoes.

Practice holding yourself in unconditional love and regard as you achieve and as you stumble in your learning to communicate with animals. Treating yourself in this way will be a huge transition into understanding the animals' worlds.

Journaling Topics

My Strengths

My Weaknesses

I vow to love myself and hold myself in complete respect, seeing I am perfect as I am with all my strengths and weaknesses. My strengths and weaknesses are personality components I called into my life so that I could learn to love more fully. These traits are not who I am essentially. Who I am essentially is LOVE.

Signed _____ Date _____

---

16. Remember that Life is a Co-created Dream

Although looking for accuracy is a method for overcoming the temptation to assume something about another without inquiry, communication will never contain the exactness of math. We are co-creating a dream every moment of our existence. What you imagine shall come to be. Co-creating ways of connecting and relating with your animal is a beautiful path. Simply bringing your heart to focus on being with your animal is the most fulfilling type of communication for both of you. One of the reasons people are so drawn to animals is that they help us to discover this.

Exercise

Sit with your animal and ask him or her to co-create a dream with you. Make notes of all you feel, see, hear, and sense when you do this.

17. Guidance From 9 Animal Friends Who Volunteered to Teach

Dove Jonah

Let the sparkles of life come to you. Close your eyes and find how magic it all is. This is the place to meet us. In the light. In the sparkles. In the magic.

Journaling Topics

Draw or paste a picture of the sparkles and the magic here to remind you of Jonah's message.

Feline Jessie

Sometimes, to know what another person has to do you must try to imagine what it is like for them. To understand us take some time at night to look at the stars. Then you will see clearly. We ask the stars questions because those are our ancestors. We need to get rest and drink good water or milk. Many people are crazy about us because of how we look and act but sometimes those people are strangers to themselves. Get to know yourself first, the stars second, and us too, because we will find you and help you this way. Then you will know we are all one.

Journaling Topics

My experience of speaking to the stars and then listening to them for advice:

Canine Charcoal Beauty

Always call out to the stars. The world of humans might mix you up if you are gone too long so call to the stars. Bark out loud and shine out who you really are for all to see. You will know each other better this way (sends an image of himself on a mound looking out at the ocean and calling to the stars with barks).

Journaling Topics

Some ways I could allow myself to simply express. Circle the ones that suit you.

play music   sing   breathe deeply   laugh a lot   cry   walk   run   give a complement   make a request   have a heart-to-heart talk   share everything that makes you happy or sad   say a prayer   meow   massage   cuddle   bark   garden   shake your body   chant   make arbitrary sounds   add your own

Red-tailed Hawk

      The mystery is no longer a ways away. You need not travel. We have come close to your home to take you back. Let me be in your heart. Let me find you. You shall cherish each other more when you learn to take yourself on the ride we offer through our wings at sunset.

Journaling Topics

My experience of listening/feeling or looking for the red-tailed hawk in my own heart

Several Dolphin Pods in Unison and Collaboration

Come here. We can truly guide you. We guide through vibrations that are like waves of light and sound. These vibrations touch the core of your heart and are music to even those who are troubled souls. Come walk our walk and talk our talk a while. Learn to trust. Learn to look deep down into the mirror where all that was lost comes to the surface again to rise and fall. You won't fall down. Listen to the music. Trust and dance. We believe what we see though we see far ahead into time that is yet to come. You can walk miles with us or alone on the sand but know you are not alone. We have come to guide you back to Nirvana.

Journaling Topics

What does the dolphin's message inspire in me?

A Whale Named Color Fuente

Tune into the rhythm embodied in the center of the earth where all is ONE. It can't be described. It is.

Journaling Topics

Do I feel this place in me?

Exercise

Sit alone in the bathtub and call the whale to bring you the oneness awareness.

Call through your heart. Call in gratitude. Call in patience. Call in love.

What I experienced.

Aspects of my experience for which gratitude is evoked in me

Elder Feline Shera

Going home must occur through walking in the body while being somewhere else where it is not crowded and there is not a lot of shuffle. When we go way back to our roots and let our bodies be our guides we discover everything ever written in any book. We contemplate the question of time and we transform and reward ourselves back into eternal hope, bliss, and trust. Peace Be You.

Journaling Topics

> If my body was an animal friend, how would I treat my body? Am I willing to treat my body this way from now on?
>
> Your body is an animal, too. S/he needs lots of love, compassion, praise and nourishment, fresh air, exercise, good things to eat, and movement!

Feline Sno

It's okay to be a Princess or Prince if that is really what you are.

> **Journaling Topics**
>
> Am I ready to love who I am and be this wonderful being I am, fully?
>
> When I do so what will life feel like?
>
> What will each day be like?
>
> What will be different?
>
> What will be the same?
>
> Will I start now?

Spiders Jason-Jasona and Hmphfe

My, human race is beautiful. If only you could see how the intricate webs you weave glisten from afar for us to admire so much. I have a hunch that you can weave yourself back though time to the sparkling gem that melts like water in the sun and shines throughout the earth. So much love is here.

Journaling Topics

Draw or paste in a picture of beauty.

See through the spiders' eyes. Know that this beauty is you!

---

18. Be in a State of Gratitude

Animals communicate through the universal language of the heart. If the intellect is not founded in a heartfelt vibration you will not connect well with your animal. If you speak from your universal heart your animal will feel this. The quickest route to the universal heart is gratitude. Sit silently and focus on everything you can think of for which you are grateful. Notice what you feel when you focus on gratitude. Once you are in a state of gratitude, send some of that gratitude to an animal friend by focusing on him or her in your heart. Notice how this makes you feel. While this step may seem simple it is the most important step in animal communication. It is the foundation upon which all other steps will take place.

Journaling Topics

YOU END WHERE YOU BEGAN. YOUR INTENTION CIRCLES AROUND. YOU BECOME WHAT YOU INTEND. YOU ARE WHOM YOU MOST KNOW.

Now add your own wisdom.

What did I learn from my studies?

If I repeat the workbook course, what will be my intention?

What do I appreciate most about my experience of this course?

Bibliography

Amritaswarupananda, Swami

Ammachi: A Biography of Mata Amritanandamayi. New Leaf Distributing Company; Lithia Springs, Georgia, 1997.

Anderson, Allen, Anderson, Linda (authors) and Becker, Marty (foreword).

Angel Animals: Divine Messengers of Miracles. New World Library; Novato, California, 1999 and 2007.

Andrews, Ted

Animal-Speak: The Spiritual & Magical Powers of Creatures Great & Small. Llewellyn Publications; St. Paul, Minnesota, 1993.

Blake, Stephen R.

The Pet Whisperer: Stories About My Friends, the Animals. The Pet Whisperer Publishing Company; San Diego, California, 2003.

Boone, J. Allen

Kinship with All Life. Harper; San Francisco, California, 1954.

Browne, Sylvia

Exploring the Levels of Creation. Hay House Inc; Carlsbad, California, 2006.

Brunke, Dawn Baumann

Animal Voices, Animal Guides: Discover Your Deeper Self through Communication with Animals. Bear & Company; Rochester, Vermont, 2009

Brunke, Dawn Baumann

Animal Voices: Telepathic Communication in the Web of Life. Bear & Company; Rochester, Vermont, 2002.

Brunke, Dawn Baumann

Shapeshifting with our Animal Companions; Connecting with the Spiritual Awareness of All Life. Bear & Company; Rochester, Vermont, 2008.

Byrne, Rhonda

The Secret. Simon & Schuster Inc; New York, 2006.

Curtis, Anita

. *Animal Wisdom: Communications with Animals.* iUniverse; Bloomington, Indiana, 1996.

De Dan, Rose

Tails of a Healer: Animals, Reiki and Shamanism. AuthorHouse; Bloomington, Indiana, 2008.

Fitzpatrick, Sonya

Cat Talk: The Secrets of Communicating with Your Cat. The Berkley Publishing Group; New York, 2003.

Grace, Raymon

>The Future is Yours: Do Something About It. Hampton Roads Publishing; Charlottesville, Virginia, 2003.

Grandin, Temple and Johnson, Catherine

>*Animals in Translation: Using the Mysteries of Autism to Decode Animal Behavior.* Simon & Schuster; New York, 2005.

Grandin, Temple and Johnson, Catherine

>*Animals Make Us Human: Creating the Best Life for Animals.* Houghton Mifflin Harcourt Publishing; Orlando, Florida, 2009.

Gurney, Carol

>*The Language of Animals: 7 Steps to Communicating with Animals.* Random House; New York, 2001.

Kinkade, Amelia

>*Straight from the Horse's Mouth: How to Talk to Animals and Get Answers. Crown Publishers,* Random House Inc; New York, 2001.

Kowalski, Gary

>*The Souls of Animals.* New World Library; Novato, CA., 1991.

Lee, Patrick Jasper

We Borrow the Earth: An Intimate Portrait of the Gypsy Folk Tradition and Culture. Thorsons; Wellingborough, England, 2000. (Republished by Ravine Press, 2013. Available through Amazon Digital Services, Inc.)

Masson, Jeffrey Moussaieff and McCarthy, Susan

When Elephants Weep: The Emotional Lives of Animals. Dell Publishing; New York, 1995.

McElroy, Susan Chernak

Animals as Teachers and Healers: True Stories and Reflections. The Ballantine Publishing Group; New York, 1996.

Mews, Anna Clemence and Dicker, Julie

What Horses Say: How to Hear, Help and Heal Them. Trafalgar Square Publishing; North Pomfret, Vermont, 2004.

Meyer, Judy

The Animal Connection: A Guide to Intuitive Communication With Your Pet. Penguin Group; New York, 2000.

Moore, Laurie and Joy, Jessie Justin

111 Messages to Humanity from Jessie Justin Joy, a Cat. Alison Frandeen Press; California, 2005.

Moore, Laurie

The Cat's Reincarnation and Unconditional Trust in Love. Alison Frandeen Press; California, 2007.

Moore, Laurie

Animiracles DVD. Alison Frandeen Press; California, 2007 (Revised 2013).

Moore, Laurie

Indimiracles DVD. Alison Frandeen Press; California, 2007.

Moss, Cynthia and Attenborough, David

Echo of the Elephants. Thirteen/WNET and BBC-TV; New York, 2006.

Ocean, Joan

Dolphins into the Future. A Dolphin Connection Book; Hawaii, 1997.

Ogden-Avrutik, Kim

Ask the Animals: Life Lessons Learned as an Animal Communicator. Lantern Books; Herndon, Virginia, 2003.

Osborn, Arthur

Ramana Maharshi and the Path of Self-Knowledge. Lightning Source Inc.; La Vergne, Tennessee, 2006.

Palmer, Gina

Paws & Claws Newsletter. Paws and Claws Sanctuary; Carlsbad, California, 2001–2006.

Person, Carla

> *Speak to My Heart* DVD. Coccora Press; Glendale, Arizona, 2004.

Person, Carla with Johnson, Hillary

> *The Calico Shaman: True Tales of Animal Communication.* Coccora Press; Glendale, Arizona, 2004.

Powell, Yael and Powell, Doug

> *Magic Cat (an enlightened animal) Explains Creation.* Circle of Light Press; Eureka Springs, Arkansas, 2004.

Ranquet, Joan

> *Communication with All Life: Revelations of an Animal Communicator.* Hay House, Inc.; Carlsbad, California, 2007.

Regan, Trish

> *Essential Joy: Finding It, Keeping It, Sharing It. Book One: The Art of Balance.* Essential Joy; Kealakekua Bay, Hawaii, 2002.

Regan, Trish

> *Essential Joy: Finding It, Keeping It, Sharing It. Book Two: Surrender to Magnificence.* Essential Joy; *Kealakekua* Bay, Hawaii, 2002.

Reynolds, Rita M.

Blessing the Bridge: What Animals Teach Us About Death, Dying, and Beyond. NewSage Press; Troutdale, Oregon, 2000.

Sibley, Meg

Dolphin Notes: Insights from My First Summer with the Dolphins. Meg Sibley; Kealakekua Bay, Hawaii, 2008.

Smith, Penelope

Animal Talk: Interspecies Telepathic Communication. Beyond Words Publishing Inc; Hillsboro, Oregon and Atria Books, a division of Simon & Schuster; New York, NY. 1978, 1989, 1999, 2008.

Smith, Penelope

When Animal's Speak: Techniques for Bonding with Animal Companions. Beyond Words Publishing Inc; Hillsboro, Oregon and Atria Books, a division of Simon & Schuster; New York, NY. 1993, 1999, 2004, 2009.

Smith, Penelope

Animals in Spirit: Our Faithful Companions' Transition to the Afterlife. Beyond Words Publishing Inc; Hillsboro, Oregon and Atria Books, a division of Simon & Schuster; New York, NY. 2008.

Smith, Penelope

Animal Communication Mastery Series (CD Set). Anima Mundi Incorporated; Prescott, AZ. 1985, 1994, 2006.

Smith, Penelope

How to Communicate with Animals—The Basic Course (CD set). Anima Mundi Incorporated; Prescott, AZ. 2004.

Smith, Penelope

Animal Healing Power (CD). Anima Mundi Incorporated; Prescott, AZ. 1994, 2008.

Smith, Penelope

Telepathic Communication with Animals (DVD). Hartworks, Inc; Crestone, CO. 1990, 2005.

Smith, Penelope

Species Link: The Journal of Interspecies Telepathic Communication. Galde Press; Lakeville, MN. Since 1990.

Steiger, Brad and Steiger, Sherry Hansen

Animal Miracles: Inspirational and Heroic True Stories. Adams Media Corporation; Avon, Massachusetts, 1999.

Steiger, Brad and Steiger, Sherry Hansen

Cat Miracles. Adams Media Corporation; Avon, Massachusetts, 2003.

Summers, Patty

> *Talking with the Animals.* Hampton Roads Publishing; Charlottesville, Virginia, 1998.

Upton, Nick (director)

> *Little Creatures Who Run the World.* Nova/PBS; Boston, Massachusetts, 1998.

Verma, Roop

> *Harmonie* (CD). Pegasus, France, 2009.

von Kreisler, Kristin

> *The Compassion of Animals: True Stories of Animal Courage and Kindness.* Three Rivers Press; New York, 1999.

Williams, Marta

> *Ask Your Animal: Resolving Behavioral Issues Through Intuitive Communication.* New World Library; Novato, California, 2008.

Williams, Marta

> *Beyond Words: Talking with Animals and Nature.* New World Library; Novato, California, 2005.

Williams, Marta

Learning Their Language: Intuitive Communication with Animals and Nature. New World Library; Novato, California, 2003.

Wright, Machaelle Small

Behaving as if The God in All Life Mattered. Perelandra Ltd.; Warrenton, Virginia, 1997.

Additional Writings

The Holy Bible Old Testament

The Holy Bhagavad Gita

The Holy Quran

Prayers of St. Francis

Online Bibliography

www.Amma.org

www.dragonhawkpublishing.com

www.thepetwhisperer.com

www.animalshealing.com

www.animalvoices.net

www.thesecret.tv

susanmcelroy.wordpress.com

www.anitacurtis.com

www.reikishamanic.com

www.sonyafitzpatrick.com

www.raymongraceprojects.com

www.templegrandin.com

www.gurneyinstitute.com

www.ameliakinkade.com

www.uusociety.org

www.absolutewrite.com

www.jeffreymasson.com

www.animiracles.com

www.joanocean.com

www.kimogden.com

www.sophiaperennis.com

www.spirithealer.com

www.joanranquet.com

www.essentialjoy.net

www.dolphinsound.org

www.animaltalk.net

www.bradandsherry.com

www.psanimal.com

www.roopverma.com

www.martawilliams.com

www.perelandra-ltd.com

www.historyplace.com

www.labyrinthina.com/mayan.htm

www.pawsandclaws.net

www.dolphinville.com

www.youtube.com/watch?v=XUJPgaPUE40

www.talk2theanimals.net

www.pbs.org/wnet/nature/echo/index.html

http://www.annettebetcher.com/index.shtml

www.spiritofhorse.com

www.om-guru.com/html/saints/anandamayi.html

www.gangaji.org

www.oprah.com/media/20090313-tows-christian-lion

www.treehugger.com/files/2008/02/baby_hippo_mother_tortoise.php).

http://images.google.com/images?hl=en&q=tortoise+and+hippo&rlz=1W1GGLD_en&um=1&ie=UTF-8&ei=xqNOSuqkKJDGsQP3wcGqDQ&sa=X&oi=image_result_group&ct=title&resnum=4

www.youtube.com/watch?v=1JiJzqXxgxo

www.oprah.com/article/oprahshow/20090416-tows-amazing-animals/9

www.youtube.com/watch?v=-IG4kceZBWA&feature=channel

www.youtube.com/watch?v=04RZrf3-Mgo&feature=related

www.youtube.com/watch?v=31LH7ZBYgQc&NR=1

www.youtube.com/watch?v=fhHVMKYzG_s&feature=related

Animal Readings

Laurie Moore, PhD, CHT, LMFT, Animal Communicator

831-477-7007

Laurie@DrLaurieMoore.com

www.animiracles.com

Made in the USA
Middletown, DE
20 November 2015